*To Fellow sojourners who,
each in their unique way,
have touched our lives
and to those whose paths
we have yet to cross. . .*

Living in Japan

*A Guide to Living,
Working, and Traveling in Japan*

Joy Norton
and
Tazuko Shibusawa

Tuttle Publishing
Boston   Rutland, Vermont   Tokyo

This revised and expanded edition first published in 2001 by Tuttle Publishing, an imprint of Periplus Editions (HK) Ltd., with editorial offices at 153 Milk Street, Boston, Massachusetts 02109. Originally published by *The Japan Times* as *The Japan Experience: Coping and Beyond* in 1989.

Copyright © 1989 by Tazuko Shibusawa and Joy Norton; this revised and expanded edition copyright © 2001 by Joy Norton and Tazuko Shibusawa.

All rights reserved. No part of this publication may be reproduced or utilized in any form or by any means, electronic or mechanical, including photocopying, recording, or by any information storage and retrieval system, without prior written permission from Tuttle Publishing.

Library of Congress Cataloging-in-Publication Data

Norton, Joy, 1948-
    Living in Japan : a guide to living, working, and traveling in Japan / by Joy Norton and Tazuko Shibusawa.
    p.cm.
    Includes bibliographical references.
    ISBN 0-8048-3288-9 (pbk.)
    1. Japan--Social life and customs--1945- 2. Americans--Japan--History--20th century.
I. Shibusawa, Tazuko. II. Title.

DS822.5 .N697 2001
952.04--dc21   2001027066

Distributed by

North America, Latin America, Europe
Tuttle Publishing Distribution Center
Airport Industrial Park
364 Innovation Drive
North Clarendon, VT 05759-9436
Tel: (802) 773-8930
Toll free tel: (800) 526-2778
Fax: (802) 773-6993
Toll free fax: (800) 329-8885

Japan
Tuttle Publishing
RK Bldg. 2nd Floor
2-13-10 Shimo-Meguro
Meguro-Ku Tokyo 153 0064
Tel: (03) 5437 0171
Fax: (03) 5437 0755

Asia Pacific
Berkeley Books LTD
5 Little Road #08-01
Cemtex Industrial Bldg
Singapore 536983
Tel: (65) 280 1330
Fax: (65) 280 6290

05 04 03 02 01   9 8 7 6 5 4 3 2 1
Printed in the United States of America

Contents

Acknowledgments	ix
Introduction	3
1 Arrival	5
Expectations	6
Culture Shock	7
Symptoms of Culture Shock	8
The Adjustment Process	12
Why Go Through It All?	15
Social Readjustment Rating Scale	16
2 Settling In	19
The U-Curve of Cultural Adjustment	19
The Family	21
Married Couples	22
Non-Married Couples	27
Children	28
Adolescents	30
Family Additions	32
Singles	33
3 Blending In	35
Loneliness	36
Making a Home	37
Friendships	39
Cross-Cultural Dating and Relationships	41
Japanese Schools and Universities	44
Working in Japan	46
4 Staying On	51
Adult Long-Term Residents	51
Careeer Changes	55
Children of Long-Term Residents	58

5 Coping — 67
- Becoming Aware of Your Feelings and Reactions — 68
- Accepting Your Feelings and Reactions — 70
- Sharing Your Experiences — 73
- Putting Things into Perspective — 75
- Constructive Activities — 76
- Emotional Inventory — 79
- Inventory of Personal Values — 81

6 Reaching Out — 83
- Why Not? — 83
- The Need to Be Connected — 84
- Community Resources — 85
- Orientation Programs and Services — 86
- Tokyo English Life Line (TELL) — 88
- Support Groups — 89
- Medical and Psychiatric Help — 92
- Counseling and Psychotherapy — 94

7 Departure — 97
- Reverse Culture Shock: An Overview — 97
- The W-Curve of Cultural Adjustment — 99
- Coping with Reverse Culture Shock — 103
- Leaving Japan — 105
- Being Home — 111

Afterword — 113

Additional Readings — 117

Notes — 121

Acknowledgments

This book would not have been possible without the support of the following people and institutions: Dr. Alice Cary, Dr. Takeo Doi, Ann Hargett, Erica Keirstead, Dr. Dora Lodwick, Adair Linn Nagata, Nishimachi International School, the American School in Japan, Dr. James Runsdorf, H. Van Buren, Richard and Mary Norton, and Masa and Chako Shibusawa.

We would also like to thank Dr. Linda Bell, Lisa Berg, Barbara Gewirtz, Gion Duon Simeon, and Judith Sharp for sharing their insights and experiences, and Dr. Patricia McDonald-Scott for her comments and feedback. Finally, our deepest appreciation goes to Coley Pogosian, our first editor.

Living
in Japan

Introduction

Whether or not we are aware of it, coping is something we all do. It is the way in which we interact with our environment in order to overcome problems and difficulties. In the archaic use of the word, *coping* is defined as "to meet" or "to encounter." Certainly there is not a more appropriate word to use when dealing with the process of interacting with a culture other than our own and with the problems that may result from such an encounter. As with learning any skill, the art of living abroad continually involves developing, mastering, and adjusting our coping abilities in order to successfully respond to the demands presented by a foreign country.

There is no doubt that some people are better copers than others, while those who may cope extremely well in one situation may feel vulnerable in other circumstances or at different times in their lives. Men and women have their own styles of coping, as do children and adults. People of different cultures, as represented in the expatriate community of Japan, whether North or South American, European, African, Oceanian, East or Southeast Asian, also cope in different ways.

It is no small task to write about the variety of ways in which people cope or about the kinds of problems they must cope with. Experience has shown us that the problems confronted by the expatriate community of Japan fall into the following general categories: (1) culture-specific, that is, related to living in Japan; (2) common to expatriate communities worldwide, as with culture shock; (3) related to an individual's or family's developmental-maturational stage, such as the midlife crisis; and (4) health-related, for example, as in coping with diabetes. Most people can cope with any one of these problems, but even a single obstacle can be made worse when a person has to deal with more than one category at a time or when it becomes difficult to differentiate between the problem areas.

Although a psychosocial approach deals with only one aspect of living in Japan, we believe it is an important one. We know that there is no fate worse than feeling totally alone—especially in a foreign country, without one's normal support systems. However, we believe that living in a new culture offers opportunities for growth, with its many facets—letting go in order to receive, befriending our fears to instill trust, seeing the humorous in the serious, and ultimately knowing that hope is real and despair but a moment in time.

Because we both have had the privilege of growing up in cultures other than our own and have worked with people of varied cultural backgrounds, this book rests on the combined experience of our personal and professional lives. It is our sincere wish not only that what we have to share will be informative and useful but that somewhere in these pages you may meet a kindred spirit.

Tazuko Shibusawa, Ph.D., L. C. S. W.
Joy Norton Van Buren, M.A., M.S.W.
Co-founders, Counseling International
Tokyo, Japan

1 Arrival

> *There is the odd and persistent fact that it is only after a faithful journey to a distant region, a foreign country, a strange land, that the meaning of the inner voice that is to guide our quest can be revealed to us.*
> —Heinrich Zimmer
> German scholar

"I reach for the door, but the knob is not there. I look down and there it is."

You have opened the doors to Japan. Were the doorknobs where you thought they would be? Were you expecting them to be in the same place as they are in your home country, or were you expecting sliding *shoji* (rice paper) doors?

People come to Japan with different expectations. Most arrive expecting things to be different and perhaps exotic— definitely not the same as they were back home. They know they will be living in a country where the language, food, and customs are different; where the crime rate is low but the cost of living high; where people are shoved into trains during rush hour; and where people do not display their emotions as they do in other cultures.

Most adults come prepared, at least in their mind, for some surprises, some discomfort, and some unique adventures. But no matter how well they prepare themselves, there will always be incidents or situations that will provoke unexpected reactions, such as confusion or anger, and low moments. Few people arrive expecting that they themselves will be changed by the experience. In trying to make yourself feel comfortable in this country, you will find the need to make a series of adjustments in order to make the best of your Japan experience.

Expectations

Your initial adjustment to a new country depends largely on your expectations. Even though you know you shouldn't expect things to be the same as in your home country, you probably arrived at Narita or Kansai International Airport carrying suitcases filled with subtle expectations that you were unaware of.

Some come to Japan expecting to find a country filled with polite and reserved people and are shocked to see the loud and boisterous behavior of men coming out of bars in the evening. Others may be disappointed to find small plastic bathtubs in their apartments after hearing so much about the spacious Japanese baths. For some, it is a shock to see the run-down quality of public institutions, such as schools, hospitals, and government offices, when Japan is supposed to be one of the wealthiest nations in the world.

Japan is, in fact, full of such contradictions. People seem polite and yet at times are outright rude or even cruel. They seem to be obsessed with cleanliness, and yet many places are filled with garbage and clutter. They tend to be reserved and private, and yet in some respects personal boundaries seem very vague, as when taxi drivers urinate in public. The serenity and peacefulness found in temple gardens are quickly erased by the loudspeakers of the *yakiimo* man (selling hot sweet potatoes), the right-wingers' jeeps, and the election campaign trucks. People seem to be indirect and yet direct. At times, you might be taken aback by what appears to be a very intrusive question. Japanese people may also seem to be patient and impatient, efficient and inefficient, quiet and loud, materialistic and spiritual, strict and indulgent. Such paradoxes are difficult, especially for Westerners who are more comfortable with things that are black-and-white, clear-cut, and hence "understandable." To adapt to Japan, the sojourner must develop a new thought process, one that allows the integration of two opposing viewpoints, and learn to be comfortable with, or at least tolerant of, daily contradictions.

The subtle expectation that creeps out as you unpack your luggage is that "things ought to make sense." In Japan, however, it's most likely they never will. In fact, things will begin to make sense only when you stop expecting things to make sense—another paradox for the newcomer to ponder.

> People had told me it was impossible to be totally accepted by the Japanese. I didn't believe them. I thought I could be different, and it took

me a year to find out they were right.
—Businessman with overseas experience

The inability to blend in among the Japanese is often a source of frustration for foreigners who come with the expectation of being immediately accepted. Many Japanese believe that they are an ethnically homogeneous group, and are ambivalent about accepting people of other nationalities and races into their culture. The discrimination against the Chinese and Korean residents who have lived in Japan for many generations is well known. It is said that what hinders the internationalization of Japan is not the lack of exposure to the West but the mentality that stubbornly refuses to acknowledge that Japanese culture can be understood by foreigners.

Another factor adding to these complications, especially for Westerners, is the change in Japan's status in relation to the international community. Japan is presently the only non-Western superpower. Every other country in Asia is a developing nation or a newly industrializing economy. You cannot come to Japan expecting only an exotic Asian experience. The problems seen in Japan often hit home, since they are similar to those affecting all the advanced nations of the world. You can't escape reality by living in Japan; an acute awareness of what is going on in the world is a real asset.

Many Westerners are caught off guard by the extent of Japan's modernization. Some aspects of Japan, for example, are more developed than what might exist in their own countries. Encountering advanced high-tech products (like those found in Tokyo's Akihabara district), efficient train systems, services that remain excellent for the most part, and the absence of run-down ghettoes can be a humbling experience, especially if you have not looked at your own country with a critical eye.

Culture Shock

When expectations of a foreign culture are not met, the usual reaction is disappointment, frustration, or anger. The individual goes through a process known as culture shock.

K. Oberg, an anthropologist, first introduced the term *culture shock*, which is used to describe reactions to something in another culture that is difficult to digest. In studying the adjustment process of anthropologists doing fieldwork in different cultures, Oberg described the experience of culture shock as an "anxiety resulting from losing one's sense of 'when to do what and how.'"[1] According to Oberg, culture shock occurs when one is unable to anticipate events accurately and does not have the control necessary to bring about an expected result.

A host of researchers have followed Oberg in studying this phenomenon, and there have been extensive studies conducted involving foreign students, scholars, and military personnel. In these studies, culture shock has been defined within the particular theoretical framework embraced by each researcher.[2]

Behavioral researchers define *culture shock* as a maladaptive response to a new situation in which an individual's previous knowledge is inadequate for coping with the new environment. Culture shock occurs because one has not learned appropriate ways to adapt to the new culture. In order to overcome culture shock, behaviorists suggest that, as quickly as possible, one acquire new skills, such as new ways of interacting with people, and learn about the new culture and its language.[3]

Psychoanalytically oriented scholars liken the experience of culture shock to the process of a child separating from the mother for the first time.[4] Thrown into an unknown environment in which one does not speak the language or understand the cultural cues, an individual experiences a helpless, childlike state. Loss of familiar surroundings can conjure up feelings like those children have when they have to let go of their mothers or give up a security blanket to which they have been clinging. According to some scholars, childhood anxieties and fears are reactivated during the process of adjusting to a new culture.[5]

No matter what the explanation, exposure and adjustment to another culture is definitely a stressful experience. New residents in a foreign land are placed in the position of having to act while being bombarded with unfamiliar or contradictory messages and cultural cues. Uncertain of the correct way to do things, newcomers often expend an exorbitant amount of energy on what would be trivial tasks in their home country.

Symptoms of Culture Shock

> I never expected I'd have difficulties here. Japan is so deceptive because it is so modern and similar to the United States. But I was so miserable in the beginning. I got lost all the time and couldn't figure out half the things they sold at the grocery store. It took me a long time before I became comfortable here.
> —Spouse of a U.S. businessman

Everyone experiences culture shock in different ways and in individual rhythms. For some it may occur right after arrival; for others it creeps up six months later, often in the form of a mild depression. It can also be a recurring experience in which the feelings of discomfort reappear after a period of smooth transition. Just as things seem to be settling down, some individuals experience the rude awakening that they are in a foreign country after all.

Observers of culture shock have identified a number of symptoms, the most frequent being a continuous, general, free-floating anxiety that affects normal behavior. Lack of self-confidence is common, and panic attacks also occur. Some people appear to lose their inventiveness and spontaneity for a period of time. Other features include excessive anger over delays and other minor frustrations, a feeling of hopelessness, and a strong desire to associate with people of their own nationality. Some find that they spend an excessive amount of time sleeping or reading, often because both activities offer sanctuary from overwhelming foreign stimuli.[6]

Distrust of others and fears that other people are taking advantage are also symptomatic of culture shock. Japan is a relatively secure country with a low crime rate, and most people do not have a pressing concern for their personal safety. When one does not understand the language (written or spoken), however, it is easy to worry about being cheated, for example at the sushi shops, where prices are often not posted.

A heightened concern over one's physical condition is a major symptom of culture shock. While some individuals become excessively concerned over minor aches and pains, we have found that a large number of people actually do become vulnerable to physical illness, such as influenza, when they first arrive in Japan. They constantly find themselves getting sick. In part, this may be due to the fact that they have not yet developed immunity to viruses common to their new environment.[7]

Unfamiliarity with the Japanese medical-care system aggravates the already stressful situation of being ill. In Japan, a visit to a hospital can mean long hours of waiting for treatment, and few doctors have a comfortable private room, as do their counterparts in the West.

There is also a marked difference in the ways in which Japanese and Western patients approach doctors. Japanese patients tend to be more passive and regard the physician as an authority figure who is not to be questioned. Westerners, however, feel it is their right to be fully informed, and the absence of information raises their anxiety level. Japanese doctors are not accustomed to patients who keep asking questions and hence are not used to answering them. This cultural difference in the approach to health care can be a source of anxiety for those with medical concerns.

There are as many symptoms of culture shock as there are observers of the phenomenon. Oberg identified six common aspects of culture shock in his seminal study: (1) strain due to the effort required to make necessary psychological adaptations; (2) a sense of loss and feelings of deprivation in regard to relationships, status, profession, and possessions; (3) being rejected by or rejecting members of the new culture; (4) confusion in one's role, role expectations, values, feelings, and self-identity; (5) surprise, anxiety, disgust, and indignation upon becoming aware of cultural differences; and (6) feelings of impotence due to an inability to cope with the new environment.

Of Oberg's six symptoms, we have found that the stress of psychological adaptation, the sense of loss, and feelings of helplessness are the three aspects most frequently reported by those who move to Japan.

Stress Mastering a new environment is a challenge even when change can be met on a predictable schedule. Getting around in a town where there are no street names or numbers, trying to learn the names of bus stops, learning the difference between a *kyuko, junkyu, kaisoku,* and *tokkyu*[6] when getting on a train, figuring out if the Japanese are saying no or yes when they nod their heads, feeling overwhelmed by the number of *kanji* (Chinese characters) to be mastered, selecting appropriate gifts when visiting someone, trying to find medicine equivalent to that used in your home country, and figuring out how to get money from the cash machine at the bank are all stressful events when you're confronted with them all at once.

The amount of energy required to accomplish everyday tasks in a new culture is enormous and exacts a toll on an individual's resources. The exhaustion that results from the number of adjustments demanded by life in a foreign country is known as "culture fatigue." Becoming the object of unsolicited attention in public because one looks different is a stress factor frequently reported by foreigners in Japan, and repeatedly being approached for a free English lesson is an uncomfortable experience for many expatriates.

An important thing to remember about stress is that people often do not recognize the amount of stress they are under, or how quickly they may be presented with stress-provoking situations. With travel time between continents so short, there is no transition period as there once was, when it took weeks, months, or even years to reach a destination. Today travelers are expected to adapt rapidly to a new culture, literally overnight. People often expect themselves to function in the same way and at the same level that they did in their home country. They become impatient with themselves, and when they feel bad, they often fail to allow themselves a grace period for adjustment.

Sense of Loss Parting with family, friends, pets, and favorite restaurants and TV programs are just a few of the losses experienced in moving to a new country. The excitement an individual feels at the prospect of moving soon diminishes, and the move itself can be a letdown and provoke feelings of loss once the destination has been reached.

In the beginning, losses can evoke feelings of sadness and emptiness similar to those during a period of mourning. It may be difficult to invest energy in establishing new relationships and developing interests in the new culture. This is a very natural reaction, and it is important to acknowledge, express, and release these feelings.

Those who come to Japan not by choice but because they are accompanying their spouse or other family members often feel loss most intensely. Adjustment is easier for those individuals who have actively chosen to come to Japan, since they have careers or studies to occupy and distract them from experiencing feelings of privation. The accompanying spouse or family members may not have these distractions, only the feelings.

Children are also sensitive to loss. Although most overcome these feelings in a relatively short time, it is difficult for them to adjust to a new environment when they remain attached to their friends back home. Introverted children may need extra time to make new friends. For children used to larger play areas and more freedom within those areas, Japan's lack of open space can be a great loss. They cannot understand why children are not permitted to run on the grass in most Japanese parks. Issues concerning the adjustment of children and adolescents are discussed further in Chapter 2.

Feelings of Helplessness An American woman who has lived in Japan for a year echoed the feelings of many other foreigners here:

> When I came to Japan, all of a sudden I felt like a child again. Back home I'd been doing well. I was successful as an account executive. I was independent. I was able to do anything I wanted. And then I came here and I couldn't even read the signs. I had to depend on someone to show me how

to get my dry cleaning done. I felt completely helpless, which was such a terrible feeling.

In the beginning, the language seems impossible to comprehend, and trying to function without being able to communicate is an extremely stressful experience. Relying on others to get things done, and thus losing a measure of independence and a sense of mastery over the environment, leads to feelings of anger, frustration, and, sometimes, depression.

The Adjustment Process

The methods employed and the ease with which individuals adjust to life in Japan depend on a number of different factors. An individual's reasons for coming here are of primary importance, but nationality, ethnicity, cultural and educational background, financial status, marital status, age, and sex all play a role in cultural adjustment.

An individual's previous life experiences also contribute significantly to the process. For example, a family transplanted directly to Tokyo or Osaka from a small suburb in the United States or Europe will have different adjustment experiences than a family who has had previous postings in other cities in Asia. The move for both families may be stressful, but the former must adjust to living in a large urban center as well as a new culture, while the latter may be used to city life in Asia and know what living in a different culture entails.

The accessibility of a support network as well as an individual's economic status have an impact on the adjustment process. There is a substantial difference in the financial status of a person sent to Japan by a corporation or an organization (e.g., diplomatic, military, religious, or academic) and those who are hired locally by Japanese companies.

Those transferred to Japan by corporations or organizations are usually sent here for a specific period of time, usually three years for North Americans and four to five years for Europeans. They receive what are known as "expat benefits," which often include subsidized housing and paid annual home leaves, and are generally more protected from the high living costs that confront other foreigners. In fact, their standard of living in Japan is often higher than in their home country. Furthermore, they usually have access to an "expat support network" and the added support of a Japanese office assistant who can help out with personal matters as well.

In contrast to the subsidized expatriates' circumstances are those of the local hires or students, who do not have these types of benefits. They rarely have access to an already existing "expat support network," and as a result, they can find themselves more isolated. They have to rely solely on their own individual resources, a situation that makes a comfortable adjustment difficult to achieve.

The degree of comfort an individual experiences in Japan is also affected by the way that person is perceived by the Japanese. There is a big difference between the ways Japanese people react to Westerners and non-Westerners. Ever since the Meiji era (1868–1912), the Japanese have looked up to Westerners. Even though economically Japan has supposedly "caught up with" and is about to "surpass" the West, many Japanese still tend to believe in Western superiority.

To most Japanese people, "Westerner" means Caucasian. Many Japanese lack sensitivity toward non-Caucasian Americans, and this is seen in their treatment of members of ethnic minorities, such as Asians, Latinos, and African Americans. The Japanese often perceive them in accordance with stereotypes similar to those found in other countries. Thus, some Westerners in Japan find themselves treated with more respect and privileges than in their own culture, whereas others find they are treated with less respect. For some people of color, interacting within the "international expat community" can pose challenges as well. Outside of the military and embassy communities, people of color tend to be underrepresented among the expats. One Filipina American who worked as an attorney in Tokyo found it very difficult to interact with the expat community because the majority of Filipinas in Tokyo are domestic workers, and she found that she constantly had to challenge the way people viewed her.

The coping skills that individuals and families bring to Japan also determine the ease with which they adjust to their new surroundings. Is an individual able to tolerate loneliness or able to seek help when there are warning signals that indicate the need for outside help? Does a family have enough flexibility to meet the changing needs of their children while providing firm rules and guidelines for them?

Often people do not seek help until there is a full-blown crisis. The decision to seek help or not is affected by an individual's cultural attitude; for example, few Europeans seek therapy. A Swiss woman who has lived in Japan for the past fifteen years attributes this difference in attitude to her belief that Europeans tend to be more self-sufficient and tolerant of psychic pain and view seeking outside help as a weakness.

The individual's age and stage of life also influence adjustment skills. Adolescents often have the hardest time adjusting to Japan, especially if they resisted their parents' relocation. Part of the problem lies in the fact that their coping styles are often difficult for adults to understand. When teenagers feel depressed, they sometimes become "hyper" in order to avoid feeling the depression, and they begin to act out: fighting with their parents, sneaking off to discos in Roppongi (a district in Tokyo with a high concentration of bars and nightclubs), shoplifting, and becoming restless and irritable. In contrast, when adults are depressed, they tend to become lethargic and display dysphoric moods, such as sadness and a sense of helplessness. As a result, the teens' coping styles are misunderstood, and they are punished for their rebellious behavior instead of being given a sympathetic ear.

Attitudes and feelings about one's own culture are factors in the process of adjusting to Japan. These attitudes can be expressed in two extreme approaches to living in a foreign culture. One is to "go native"; the other is to "never leave home."

Those who "go native" have a tendency to idealize Japan. They fall in love with everything that is Japanese and reject many qualities of their own culture. A typical example is the person who comes to study an aspect of Japanese culture, such as the martial arts, religion, or philosophy, and eventually falls victim to depression and disillusionment when things fall short of his or her expectations and standards.

Those who "never leave home" try to maintain the lifestyle they had in their own culture. They have a tendency to idealize their own culture and are reluctant to accept the new values and ideas they are exposed to in Japan. Eventually, however, these individuals find that it is impossible to "never leave home," regardless of how much they immerse themselves in the expatriate subculture.

Everyone is changed by the mere experience of moving away from home and facing the challenge of living as a foreigner. The trauma for those who "never leave home" occurs during home leave or, perhaps worse, when they finally return home. They discover, to their dismay, that home is not as perfect as they had imagined it to be. This phenomenon, known as "reverse culture shock," is discussed in Chapter 7.

A Social Readjustment Rating Scale for adults is found on page 16. This test is based on the premise that the levels of stress individuals experience are affected by the number of life changes they simultaneously undergo.

Life events that may have occurred during the past year are listed according to the degree of severity of the accompanying stress. Generally, those who score over 300 points are vulnerable to stress-related problems. People who move to Japan generally score at least 350 points. The test will help you see the number of changes involved in moving to another country and the amount of stress you may be subjected to because of them.

In addition, some must cope with changes inherent in the life cycle, such as having children for the first time or seeing children leave home for college. Known as "cluster stress," this occurs when an individual is confronted with several major changes at the same time. For example, a new "blended family" who moves to Japan not only has to adjust to a new culture but must also get used to one another, the new marriage, and new parenting roles while coping with the losses of the first marriage and family. In addition to these stress factors, the parents may be going through a midlife crisis, while the children are facing the turmoil of reaching puberty.

Why Go Through It All?

With all the stress encountered in the adjustment to another culture, you might begin to ask if this experience is really worth all the trouble. Most of those who go through it would say emphatically, "Yes!" Many of them have found the following to be some of the positive benefits of their stay in Japan:

Increased family cohesiveness

Increased opportunity to travel to different countries

Increased opportunity to meet and establish relationships with a wide range of people and the ability to establish rapport with others more easily

Development and pursuit of new interests

Development of leadership skills through participation in various organizations

Increased objectivity about one's own culture

Increased self-understanding

Increased opportunities to reevaluate personal values

Increased self-confidence

Expanded worldview

Increased flexibility and patience

Enhanced ability to set reasonable standards of success

Tolerance for divergent points of view
Increased cultural diversity and sensitivity toward minorities
Increased creative problem-solving abilities

Others:
_____
_____
_____

There are probably many more benefits to be added to this list. The blank spaces are there for you to add items from your own life. We have found that most people make the best of the Japan experience. When they leave, their suitcases, once filled with unrealistic expectations, are now filled with positive memories and a sense of accomplishment.

Social Readjustment Rating Scale[9]

Score yourself on the life change test. If any of the events in the Life Event column have occurred in the past twelve months, enter the Item Value in the Your Score column.

Item No.	Item Value	Your Score	Life Event
1	100	_____	Death of spouse
2	73	_____	Divorce
3	65	_____	Marital separation
4	63	_____	Jail term
5	63	_____	Death of a close family member
6	53	_____	Personal injury or illness
7	50	_____	Marriage
8	47	_____	Fired at work
9	45	_____	Marital reconciliation
10	45	_____	Retirement
11	44	_____	Change in health of a family member
12	40	_____	Pregnancy
13	39	_____	Sex difficulties
14	39	_____	Gain a new family member
15	39	_____	Business readjustment

Item No.	Item Value	Your Score	Life Event
16	38	_____	Change in financial state
17	37	_____	Death of a close friend
18	36	_____	Change to different line of work
19	35	_____	Change in number of arguments with spouse
20	31	_____	Mortgage over $10,000
21	30	_____	Foreclosure of mortgage or loan
22	29	_____	Change in responsibilities at work
23	29	_____	Child leaving home
24	29	_____	Trouble with in-laws
25	28	_____	Outstanding personal achievement
26	26	_____	Wife begins or stops work
27	26	_____	Begin or end school
28	25	_____	Change in living conditions
29	24	_____	Revision of personal habits
30	23	_____	Trouble with boss
31	20	_____	Change in work hours or conditions
32	20	_____	Change in residence
33	20	_____	Change in schools
34	19	_____	Change in recreation
35	19	_____	Change in church activities
36	18	_____	Change in social activities
37	17	_____	Mortgage or loan less than $10,000
38	16	_____	Change in sleeping habits
39	15	_____	Change in number of family get-togethers
40	15	_____	Change in eating habits
41	13	_____	Vacation
42	12	_____	Christmas
43	11	_____	Minor violations of the law

*Your Total Score for Twelve Months _____

2 Settling In

With each full moon I view
Let me count the mountains
That look like those of home.
　—Issa
　　Japanese poet

The children have settled into school and no longer ask when they get to go back home. You no longer feel or look like a tourist. In fact, even Japanese are asking you for directions. By now you may have discovered you do not like *natto* (fermented soybeans), but miso soup for breakfast is palatable. You've learned how to avoid weekend crowds and found areas that offer solace, such as out-of-the-way coffee shops or temple grounds. You know many *hiragana* (the cursive *kana* of the Japanese syllabary) by heart and recognize several kanji. You are even making travel plans for your first vacation after surviving a major holiday or birthday away from relatives and close friends. With a few modifications, you have now begun to feel settled in your new surroundings.

The U-Curve of Cultural Adjustment

In looking back over the past six months, you may find you have experienced some very low moments, but things are looking up now. Studies indicate that people go through three phases when settling down in a foreign country. This is known as the "U-curve hypothesis of cultural adjustment."[1] In figure 1, the bold horizontal line depicts the baseline level of emotions—the so-called balanced state when one is not in crisis.

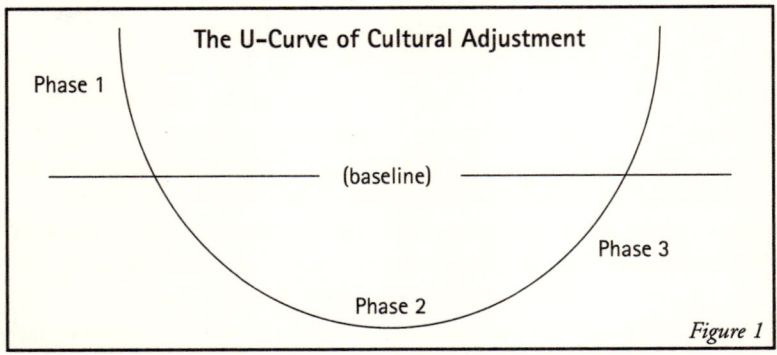

Figure 1

During Phase 1, people learn they will be moving to another country. This phase, which includes the period prior to departure and immediately after arrival, is usually associated with positive feelings. Upon learning they will be moving to another country, many people experience feelings of excitement and anticipation. Even those who are reluctant to move get caught up in the excitement of attending good-bye parties and watching others' excitement about the move. Once they arrive, the novelty effect prevails and everything is new and interesting. Any negative aspects and worries tend to be pushed aside during this "honeymoon" period, which usually lasts about two to three months.

Sometime between three and six months, however, the novelty begins to wear off. During Phase 2, things that were previously considered exotic become sources of frustration. There is general dissatisfaction with daily living, and conflicts and negative feelings appear as the individual is forced to make adjustments to things that are difficult to accept about the new home. The person becomes vulnerable to anxiety and depression during this phase, and it is considered to be the lowest period during the sojourn. Sluzki, a family therapist who has studied migrant families in the United States, found that families usually experience the shock and effects of migrating to a new country beginning about the sixth month following relocation.[2]

Phase 3 finds the process of adjustment beginning after six to eight months. As newcomers gain some mastery over the language and learn the social norms, they are able to function more adequately, at least in the daily routine. There is a reevaluation of the culture, and individuals learn to appreciate what they like and to tolerate or ignore what is unacceptable. There is also an integration of the foreigner/stranger roles during this phase.

The Family

The U-curve model enables us to understand the various phases of adjustment to a new culture. From our experience, however, we find that people do not always go through these stages in the order described. In fact, in our work with couples and families, we find that the differences in style and pace of adjustment of each group member are what often create tension in the family.

Men, usually the ones who bring their families to Japan, tend to come with high expectations. They go through the honeymoon period initially and then become discouraged when faced with difficulties at work. The lack of understanding and interest from the home office, difficulties with the Japanese staff and clients, and complaints from family members are some of the factors that elicit feelings of discouragement and helplessness. Women may also follow the typical pattern, especially if it was their own careers that brought them to Japan. For both working men and women, there are temptations during the honeymoon phase to desire or actually make changes at work, believing that one's professional knowledge and experience is the latest, best, or most efficient way of doing things. Such enthusiasm and good intentions can unintentionally alienate superiors, colleagues, and staff members, whose negative reactions cause additional stress during the culture-shock phase.

Those who accompanied their spouses to Japan may experience ambivalence, especially if they were not initially eager to move. They may not experience the honeymoon phase but go directly to Phase 2 (figure 1). This can create tensions in the marriage if one spouse is relatively happy and unaware of, or disappointed in, the other spouse's dissatisfaction.

The manner in which children experience the adjustment phase usually depends on their age. Children under three years of age are usually unaffected by the move, although they may be affected by the tension experienced by other family members. Kindergarten and elementary-school-age children may not experience Phase 1, since they are often preoccupied with their immediate surroundings, such as school and family life, rather than the larger culture around them. Some children display immediate difficulties in adjusting to the new environment, particularly at school. The young child's transition to Phase 3 sometimes occurs in a much shorter time span compared with that of an adult.

Personality styles and characteristics affect the ease with which children adjust to any new situation. Extroverted children usually have an easier time than introverted ones. Sibling rivalry may be intensified during this time if one child seems to be adjusting better than the other. While most parents are aware of the different personality styles of their children, it is important to bear in mind how this may affect their adjustment process and to refrain from placing undue expectations on them. Tensions in the family can arise when parents are unaware of the different adjustment phases each child is experiencing.

Adolescents seem to display one of two widely divergent models of adjustment to Japan. Some dislike the country from the very beginning and experience many difficulties, while others seem to thrive in the new environment to the point that they have great difficulty readjusting when they return home. Some, like typical teenagers, will not admit they are enjoying Japan even if they are. The adolescents' adjustment is largely dependent upon finding a peer group within which they feel comfortable.

Married Couples

> This has been such a great experience for my husband and me. It's so good to have someone to talk to when you're feeling down, and to have someone who understands exactly what you're going through. I think we've really gotten close, and we find we work so well together.
> —Schoolteacher who teaches with her huband

> I was so miserable when I got here. My kids would go off to school in the morning and then I'd feel so lost and overwhelmed. I'd tell my husband but he wouldn't listen, and then I'd feel so alienated. It was just awful. It wasn't until I found a part-time job that I started to feel normal again.
> —Wife of a corporate businessman

As these statements illustrate, there is no fixed pattern in the cultural adjustment process, and individuals experience adjustment in different ways. Some marriages seem to be strengthened by the process, and others experience a crisis.

Couples who have similar interests and pursue common goals while living in Japan—whether it is learning about the culture, being active in an organization, enjoying family life, or working toward common financial goals—find their relationship enriched by their stay here. Those who share responsibilities, rather than adhere to prescribed roles, are also able to develop more empathy toward each other's adjustment process.

Causes for potential marital conflicts can best be understood by looking at different roles spouses assume after moving to Japan. According to Sluzki, the role differences between spouses become more pronounced when they move to another country.[3] The husband and wife begin to assume roles that may be in direct opposition to each other.

The husband who moves into a new culture with a job must adjust to his surroundings as quickly as possible. Consequently, his interests center on the tasks of cultural adjustment. Many husbands become absorbed in learning the Japanese language and culture and invest their energy in attending business meetings and engagements until late into the night. This is in addition to making frequent business trips both within and outside of Japan. In some cases, the husband or father is hardly at home. It can seem to family members that all he does is either get ready for his next trip or recover from the last one.

The wife, as the anchor for the family, tries to minimize the loss and soften the impact of the move, acting as a bridge between the new country and what the family left behind. She tries to provide a comfortable home for her husband and children by preparing their favorite dishes that she used to serve back home and by preserving, as much as possible, the lifestyle and customs they had in their home country. Even though she herself may be more interested in trying her newest Japanese recipes, the children's demands for familiar foods can force her to place her own interests on the back burner. In her attempt to keep her family happy, the wife tends to stay connected to the familiar culture, while the husband is focused on connecting to the new one. In many ways they find their roles tugging them in opposite directions.

The lack of understanding and credit given to mothers is another cause of potential problems. Mothers, in fact, are the greatest heroines of the overseas experience. Reportedly, it is the wife who "often pays the greatest price" for the family's move.[4] She is expected to be a superwoman who provides the most: namely, support to her husband, who might be cranky after a hard day at the office; comfort to their children, who may be having difficulties at their new school; maintenance of an orderly household; adaptation to her husband's frequent business trips; and, in the case of the corporate wife, playing the role of the impeccable hostess when her husband's boss is in town. In addition to these demands, she is also expected to be happily pursuing her own interests and enthusiastically learning about the new culture and the language. At the same time, there are few places where she can receive positive reinforcement for all her efforts. It is especially difficult for the woman who has given up her own career to accompany her husband to Japan. Switching from "Hello, I'm so-and-so and I do such-and-such" to "Hello, I'm so-and-so and my husband works for such-and-such" can be a depressing experience, as the wife's identity becomes blurred with that of her husband and his company. Some women have had to interrupt fulfilling careers back home as physicians, teachers, attorneys, nurses, social workers, and corporate executives and worry about whether they will be able to pick up from where they left off professionally. Many women find it difficult to become "dependent" on their spouses, both financially and in terms of their visas. One attorney who had just gone through Phase 2 of the U-Curve remarked:

> Until I realized no one held a gun to my head to get me to come here, for the first seven months I really resented my husband for having a job. I absolutely refused to see that he sympathized with my plight, but that he was so overwhelmed with his work and he couldn't support what I was going through. And all I did was make him feel so guilty for how I was feeling.

In families receiving expat benefits, the husband often assumes that the live-in help and increase in financial benefits will allow his wife to pursue her interests and to travel frequently. He assumes that she has an easier life in Japan than she had in their home country. Consequently, he often does not understand his wife's dissatisfaction.

His wife, however, may resent her husband for his perception of her life. She feels that she made the greater sacrifice in moving to Japan and that it is she who has kept the family together. Her husband, preoccupied with business concerns, is often unavailable to listen to her complaints and may be resentful when she seems dissatisfied.

The "distancer-pursuer sequence" postulated by T. Fogarty, a family therapist, is a useful tool in understanding the marital conflicts that may occur when moving to another culture. According to Fogarty, there are two ways in which people react to stress: one is to reach out to other people in order to alleviate anxieties; the other is to distance themselves from people and to become involved with activities or hobbies that require little interpersonal contact. The former is called the "emotional pursuer" while the latter is called the "emotional distancer."[5]

Distancer–Pursuer Interactional Sequence

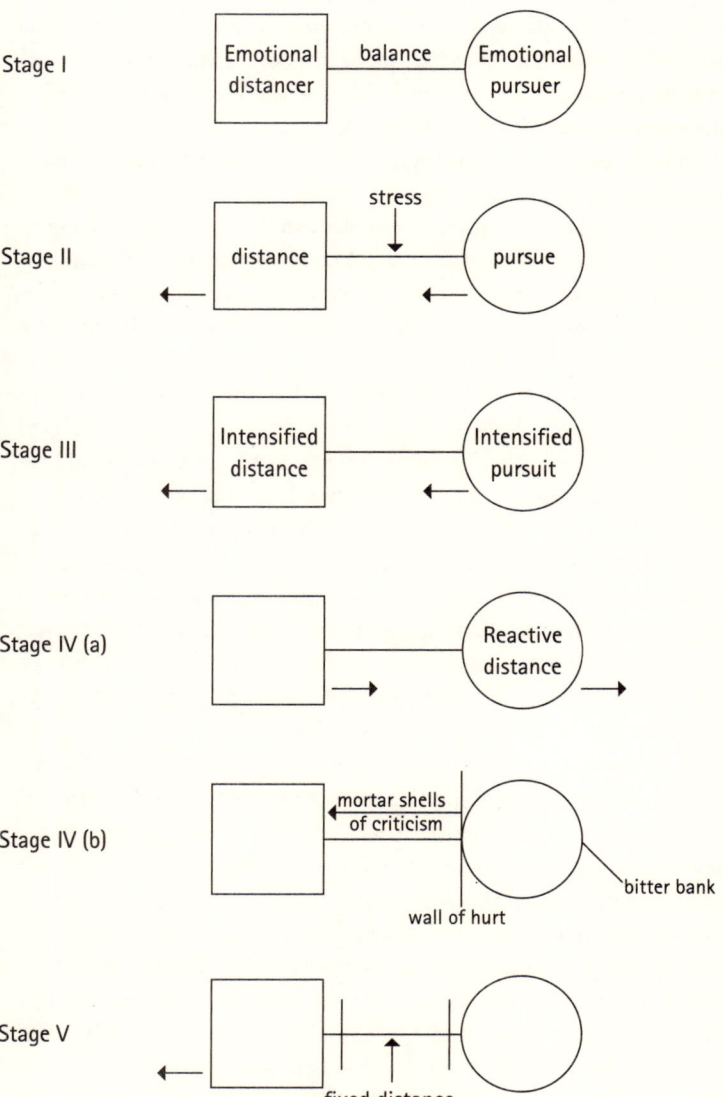

Figure 2

Figure 2 illustrates what happens in an interaction between an emotional distancer and pursuer when the pair experiences stress. In our practice, we have often found that the wife usually displays the characteristics of the emotional pursuer and the husband displays those of the emotional distancer, but this is not always the case. In the following example, the square represents the husband and the circle represents the wife.

Stage I illustrates the couple without any stress. There is balance in their relationship.

Stage II begins when the couple experiences stress, such as in moving to another country. The pursuer seeks the solace of the distancer for reassurance in dealing with the stress. The distancer, on the other hand, withdraws himself from the situation and his spouse. Being alone is usually the most comfortable way for him to deal with stress.

In Stage III we find the wife intensifying her pursuit as her anxiety mounts in the absence of reassurance from her husband. The husband increases his distancing as his wife intensifies her pursuit. We often find husbands distancing themselves from their wives by concentrating on their work and becoming consumed by their Japanese language lessons or business dinners in the evenings and obligatory weekend golf games. At this stage, some husbands are under a lot of stress from their jobs, and some experience anxiety attacks, dizziness, or heart palpitations. The distancer tends to internalize his feelings. It is especially difficult for him to express feelings that indicate weakness, such as loneliness or helplessness. In addition to denying his own affective needs, he tends to be unaware of or unresponsive to the needs of others. The wife experiences her husband's distancing as a rejection and begins to accumulate her resentment and disappointments in what Fogarty calls a "bitter bank."[6]

In the first half of Stage IV(a), the wife begins to distance herself in response to her husband's withdrawal in what is called "reactive distance." As the wife distances herself from her husband, she begins to concentrate on other things. She may develop a negative habit, such as compulsive shopping or eating, both of which are attempts to fill an emptiness she feels inside herself. Another woman may begin to focus all her attention on her children, which may lead to a process known as "triangulation" in which the child is used by the parent to satisfy needs that are unmet by the spouse. The result is an undue burden on the child to keep the parent happy. The husband may be shaken by his wife's reactive distance at this stage and begin to pay attention to her.

In the second half of Stage IV(b), the husband changes his distancing stance to pursue his wife. She is too disappointed to accept his gestures of reconciliation and puts up a "wall of hurt." Her bitter bank has accumulated too many negative feelings, and when her husband attempts to move toward her, she fires "mortar shells of criticism" at him. As a result, the husband retreats into his distancing stance. In some instances, it is at this stage that he finds himself attracted to his Japanese secretary, language instructor, or interpreter, who seems available and willing to meet his professional and personal needs. The Japanese lover becomes a convenient escape, and he does not have to deal with "the nagging wife."

In Stage V we find a fixed distance between the couple has developed. The husband has put up his own "wall of hurt" in reaction to his wife's wall, and the couple are no longer able to communicate their emotional needs to each other.

Non-Married Couples

When going through the various phases of cultural adjustment, non-married couples experience many of the same issues as those discussed above. However, they may be affected in a different way, depending on their reasons for coming to Japan and the level of commitment of the individuals involved.

Those who have come to Japan with uncertainties about the relationship may find that the culture-shock phase of adjustment reinforces any doubts and concerns they may have had previously. This is especially true for those who have consciously or unconsciously moved overseas to push, or bring to the fore, the issue of commitment. It is equally true of those who may see the move as a trial run before making any further or permanent decisions about what direction the relationship should take. Not having various supports for "couplehood," as married couples have, the first sign of trouble may be enough to question the relationship. This may be manifested in becoming attracted to other people or, if things do not go right workwise, in thinking about being relocated or returning home.

Even couples who come to Japan with more certainty about their relationship may, for the first time, find themselves questioning or reevaluating each other and the viability of the partnership in general. All at once, such highly valued traits as being independent, self-assured, and self-directed may give way to a side of the partner's personality that had not been seen before. One woman observed:

I couldn't believe what was happening. We used to agree on almost everything, and suddenly we were disagreeing about everything. It was really scary.

Regardless of the degree of uncertainty a couple may have about the relationship, the first year in Japan should not be considered as a valid or reliable indication of the relationship's state of health or a prediction of its future success. If the couple is living together for the first time, the additional stress of adjusting to each other's daily habits must also be taken into account, especially if they are residing in a small and cramped Japanese apartment.

Children

> Therapist: Draw me a picture of your home.
> Child: My home? I can't.
> Therapist: Oh . . . ?
> Child: I don't live in a home. I live in a concrete building. There's no backyard or place to play. I don't even have a chimney. I don't even know if Santa Claus is going to find me this Christmas.

This is a conversation with a seven-year-old boy who had just moved from Australia to Japan. He was referred for counseling by his homeroom teacher because he had remained withdrawn and was having difficulty making friends.

This boy was reacting to a sense of loss, the foremost factor affecting children who have moved to another country. The idea that he may be too far away for Santa to find him portrays the child's sense of insecurity. Children react in different ways to the loss of familiar surroundings and time with extended family members, such as grandparents, uncles, and aunts, as well as to the loss of friends and pets. Some, like this boy, become withdrawn, while others express their frustration and sadness by acting out in school and displaying aggressive behaviors. From our experience, we find that boys display both aggressive and passive behaviors, whereas girls more often display passive behavior.

A change in family structure also has an impact on children. Having live-in help for the first time may be a luxury for the parents, but for some children it is perceived as a loss. They experience the domestic worker as having taken over their mother's role. When asked what their mommies do during the day, some children portray their mothers as "helping their live-in help." Others experience their mothers as being less available. The mother may be trying to make the best of her Japan experience by getting out of the house and pursuing outside interests, but the child perceives this behavior as rejection. Temper tantrums and stealing money can be indications that the child is feeling neglected.

The physical arrangements of the new home can also represent a loss to children. They no longer see their fathers doing the yard work or making repairs on the house, which gives them the impression that their fathers are no longer involved with the family. Lack of space to run around in also poses problems for children, because they have little room to release their energy or to play with their parents.

Children attending international schools sometimes find that the academic pace is too strenuous in the beginning. International schools in Japan have higher academic standards than the average public schools in countries like the United States, Canada, Australia, and New Zealand. Friendships can also be a challenge in international schools because of the high turnover rate of students. Most children, though, are able to adjust to an environment where there are constant "hellos" and "good-byes."

International schools can present non–North American children with several problems. In addition to possible language difficulties, they must get used to both Japan and to the North American curriculum and social interaction patterns. Some European, Asian, and African children experience cultural conflicts with American children in the beginning because they feel that their values are different and that the American children are too rough. Families from the United Kingdom, Australia, and New Zealand are sometimes concerned about their children becoming too immersed in American English and worry that losing their accents will pose problems for the children when they return home.

Children who attend international schools may get undue attention from some Japanese people, who will often approach foreign children to tell them how *kawaii* (cute) they are. This bothers most children in the beginning, but some come to expect this special treatment. Special attention can have positive effects in that children feel nurtured and loved. It can have negative effects, however, when children become dependent on being the focus of attention and when they feel they can manipulate adults because of their unique status.

Adolescents

As mentioned in the previous chapter, adolescents are often the family members who have the most difficult time adjusting to Japan. Not only do they have to adjust to a new environment, but they are also facing puberty, a period when they experience rapid physical changes and the accompanying mood swings. Self-conscious about their changing appearances, adolescents strive for normality, that is, to be accepted by their peers. What they least want is to stand out and be noticed, which is precisely what happens to foreigners in Japan.

In our practice, we find more middle-school-age children being referred for counseling than high school students. This is probably due to the fact that more changes take place in the child during early adolescence (eleven to fifteen years old) than in later adolescence, and these changes pose more problems for both the individual child and the parents. Adolescents are referred for counseling for a variety of problems, including academic underachievement, interpersonal-relationship problems, and acting-out behaviors such as shoplifting, lying to teachers, and truancy.

Parents often come to the office and describe their adolescents as being totally out of control and wild. When the adolescents come in, they turn out to be very sensitive, with basically decent values, and genuinely upset at themselves for having gotten into trouble. Some need time to open up, but once they do, most talk about the sadness they feel about being away from their home country, frustrations toward their parents, academic and social pressures at school, and their feelings of being "caged" in Japan.

As mentioned in Chapter 1, we have found that teenagers who have problems adjusting to Japan are more depressed than adults realize, because they express depression differently than adults do. When adolescents are depressed, they often display active behavior, such as restlessness, anxiety, irritability, fighting with adults, or running away. These "hyper" activities are ways in which teenagers avoid feeling their depressive emotions.

Depression among adolescents is characteristically very intense because they are facing so many hormonal, physical, and social changes. They are unable to pinpoint and express what they are feeling, and it is rare to have a teenager articulate feelings of depression. Adolescents often want to be helped when they feel bad, but they are unable to ask for help. By acting out, they get the attention they need.

Several factors trigger teenage depression, regardless of whether the teen lives at home or abroad. These include (1) death of a loved one, (2) separation from a loved one, (3) loss of a familiar lifestyle, (4) loss of self-esteem, (5) loss of boundaries and guidelines, (6) loss of normality, and (7) parental depression.[7] We find that adolescents who move to Japan are exposed to all of these factors, with the exception of the first one, the death of a loved one. They experience separation from their friends, and for many of them, unlike for adults, it is the first time they must confront this type of loss. The loss of a familiar way of life is unavoidable upon moving to Japan, and many lose a sense of self-esteem, which accompanies a loss of control over their environment. There is often a loss or weakening of boundaries and guidelines because of the parents' relief to be in Japan, where it is safe and relatively drug-free. They may not, however, be aware of other temptations, such as vending machines that sell alcohol, cigarettes, and pornographic magazines, and bars that allow entrance to teenage foreigners. The adolescent also experiences a loss of "normality" by the fact of being a foreigner in Japan.

Some teenagers never adjust to life in Japan. In this situation, parents must carefully consider the pros and cons of trying to force the adolescent to live here. Having a peer group is extremely important for a teen, but if it is difficult for the child to find one, then boarding school should be considered as an alternative. This also applies to adolescents who have academic difficulties, such as learning disabilities, that require special help that is not always available in Japan's international schools.

Difficulties among teenagers can pose challenges for blended families. Some adolescents express a wish to return to their home country to be with their "other parent." When this is an option, it can open up many unresolved issues from the past. It is important for families to think things through carefully, perhaps with the assistance of a family therapist, so that the decision can be experienced as a positive solution rather than as a failure on the part of the adolescent or family.

Most adolescents do, however, ultimately make peace with the fact that they live in Japan and take things in stride, even though they may not absolutely love the experience. The public transportation system and Japan's low violent-crime rate, which ensure a high degree of personal safety, give many adolescents increased mobility and a new sense of freedom. They come to appreciate a sense of autonomy they could not have achieved at such an early age in their home countries.

Family Additions

It is not uncommon during an expat's stay in Japan to experience an increase in the size of the family through birth or adoption of a child. In fact, many women find that Japan is a good place to start or add to the family. Some expat women have seen coming to Japan as an opportunity to start a family, given their new free time (especially for those who left behind a career). Many have discovered that giving birth or adopting in Japan has been a pleasant surprise because of the country's baby/child-oriented culture and its physically safe environment in which to raise a child. A prospective mother can also expect excellent pre- and postnatal care, childbirth-preparation classes in English, access to midwives, a comparatively long hospital stay (if desired) after the birth, and mother-infant play groups. In many cases, birth or adoption has provided a legitimate excuse for grandparents to come for a visit and to lend their expertise and support.

For couples who are expecting their first child, many issues will be the same here as back home, but intensified because of having to go through a new experience in an unfamiliar culture without many of the resources one would normally have. The once exclusive one-to-one relationship will have to give way to include a third member who will totally absorb the mother's time, often making the husband feel left out. When there are siblings, the youngest child will most likely need to go through a major adjustment phase, learning to deal with his or her anger at being replaced as the "baby." Keep in mind that pregnancy and gaining a new member in the family has a medium stress level, as indicated on the Social Readjustment Rating Scale (p. 16).

One major decision a family may be confronted with upon arrival in Japan is whether there is a need for household help and, if so, to what extent and from what nationality, that is, in what language. Such a consideration should not be taken lightly, as the part-time or live-in person, in addition to the practical help he or she provides, will become a cherished family member.

For those with children, live-in help has proved to be a godsend. Live-in help can become a necessity to ensure not only that children get the attention they need but also that parents are free to maintain the couple relationship. For some expat women, however, issues may also arise about how they perceive their role as wife and mother in the family vis-à-vis the live-in help. Women who do not work may have feelings of uselessness for seemingly not being able to handle the role of homemaker. A working mother may feel jealous of someone who seems to be winning the affections of her child. For those whose live-in help is non-Japanese (as in most cases), it cannot be forgotten that this new family member may also be going through the various stages of adjusting to Japan—in addition to being worried about loved ones back home or future employment in Japan.

Finally, pets must not be overlooked as legitimate members of the family. In fact, it is quite common for families to take in a stray cat or dog—most likely found by their children on the way home from school. If space permits, pets are ideal additions, not only as stress busters (as research has shown) but also in helping to offset the complexities of living abroad by their simple needs and appreciation for even the smallest amount of attention. For children, pets can be a real source of comfort and companionship and provide a chance to learn about the responsibilities of caretaking.

Singles

Like couples, singles must also go through the various stages of adjusting to life in Japan. There are, however, a few differences due to the fact that, for the most part, one is going through the adjustment process alone, with all its positive and negative effects.

For singles in Phase 1, or the "honeymoon" phase (figure 1), which includes the period prior to departure and immediately after arrival, expectations may be higher for those who have come to Japan in order to fulfill certain hopes and dreams, as opposed to those who are sponsored (usually families) and here to fulfill an assignment. Expectations are often considerably higher than usual for those who have come to Japan searching for a new career, a cross-cultural experience, or a chance to get away from a conflictive situation in their own country. Often during this first phase there can be a tendency to overlook any negative aspects of Japan, so as to justify, for themselves and others, their reason for leaving their home country, especially if they have severed any personal or professional ties back home.

Once the honeymoon phase is over, culture shock can sometimes set in for singles much earlier than for families, depending on their level of isolation. Even singles with foreign or Japanese sponsors can feel abandoned during this phase, having been given attention and support upon arrival in the form of welcoming parties and orientation programs, but then left to their own devices during the critical culture-shock phase.

While couples and families are made up of familiar people, values, assumptions, and traditions, where little effort is needed to be accepted or understood, singles lack such a ready-made support system. In addition, while couples and families serve as a buffer, shield, and safe haven between oneself and the new culture, singles—especially those living and working in a predominantly Japanese environment—are often forced to interact with the host country on a more immediate and deeper level.

Lacking the structure and support of a partner or family, singles are particularly vulnerable to becoming overinvolved in their work or in friendships or intimate relationships during the honeymoon phase, a time when one feels vulnerable emotionally. Such relationships may be unconsciously used as distractions from some of the more unpleasant side effects of Phase 2 of culture shock, like anxiety and depression. Often, once the newcomer reaches Phase 3 of his or her cultural adjustment, there can be a feeling of having outgrown many of the relationships formed upon arrival. What may have once been a lifeline can soon feel like a noose around one's neck six to eight months down the road. As one becomes less dependent on others for language and the practical aspects of settling in, one's needs and interests change or expand, and the personhood one had before the sojourn is regained. At times one finds that close relationships formed during the first six months may become more distant as time goes on.

There are advantages to going through periods of cultural adjustment alone. Unlike couples, who must think about the needs and welfare of their partner, spouse, or children, singles are responsible only for themselves. This can lessen the overall level of stress and increase one's options in dealing with adjustment-related problems if or when they arise. It is not easy, and sometimes impossible, for families to make changes regarding jobs, housing, schools, or partners or to consider returning home if things do not turn out as expected.

Because singles are often forced to have more interaction with the host culture, they also have the kind of opportunities needed in order to learn about the culture, social norms, and language of Japan—all necessary ingredients for a successful and enriching overseas experience. Of course, both couples and singles who have full expat benefits must make a conscious effort to avoid becoming too insular and isolated from the culture in which they are residing.

3 Blending In

Go into your own ground and learn to know yourself.
—Meister Eckhart
German scholar/mystic

With a sigh of relief, the first year of cultural adjustment is well behind you. Feeling settled, you may even be putting down a few roots in your new environment—some of which may be coming into contact with Japanese culture. However much you may have come to terms with Japan, there will still be aspects of the culture that you may never be able to ignore, tolerate, integrate, or accept. Although you may find that your reactions can be rationally understood (e.g., why Japanese usually bow instead of shake hands, embrace, or kiss when greeting a friend), you may realize that the act of bowing will never be satisfying for you on a "gut" or emotional level. In essence, the process of blending in with a new environment may mean that some of the ingredients you bring to the "cultural melting pot" may never mix smoothly—even with your best efforts.

Such a reality should not be looked upon as a failure to adjust, but rather as a normal process of better understanding and appreciating who we are as individuals and as members of a particular culture. Irritations, frustrations, and disappointments often tell us more about ourselves than the "different" or "offending" culture. By knowing ourselves, we can then better differentiate between situations that have more to do with our own psychological makeup and background than with the foreign culture.

This chapter discusses the kinds of challenges sojourners often face when encountering Japanese culture. Although to some extent all expats in Japan are in contact with the culture, some people may find themselves in more consistent and immediate contact than others. This is particularly true of those who are single, work as local hires in foreign companies or are in Japanese work environments, date or are married to Japanese nationals, attend Japanese schools or universities, or live outside of major cities.

Loneliness

While most expats expect a certain amount of loneliness when living in a foreign environment, those involved in Japanese society to a greater degree often say that they have a little more of it than they are used to, or wish to have. If "feeling lonely" or "being alone" is thought of as something to be feared, denied, ashamed of, or too embarrassing to talk about, the "problem" of loneliness can then be compounded. Held by many Westerners, such an attitude is in direct contrast to the more philosophical, poetic Japanese notion of *sabishisa,* or loneliness, which openly acknowledges the premise that humankind is ultimately alone. Being acutely sensitive to the various nuances of being *sabishii* (lonely), many Japanese will often unabashedly ask whether you are lonely if you live alone, are single, have only one child, have a spouse who is away, or live in the countryside without another house in sight. Many foreigners feel that such questions are an invasion of their privacy, when, in fact, their Japanese interrogators are only expressing their own general feelings of loneliness in the hope of finding someone to commiserate with.

To handle feelings of loneliness, some expats may find themselves reacting in either of the ways discussed below. Ideally one should strive for a balance between the two, as both reactions are necessary for our adjustment and growth in Japan.

One reaction is to become consumed by the hectic pace of the Japanese lifestyle, leaving little room for relationships, relaxation, and reflection. Before one fully realizes what is happening, it is not uncommon to find oneself overextended. This is particularly true in the area of work, which can often serve as a surrogate family—in Japan, in fact, it strives to perform such a function. Even in leisure there can be much frenetic activity, whether it be joining clubs, taking courses, traveling in and out of Japan, partying, or exercising. The busy lifestyle can lead to unhealthy eating and sleeping habits, leaving some more vulnerable to illnesses. Such busyness can also be used as a way to avoid having to come into contact with Japanese culture, for those preferring familiar routines and patterns rather than new experiences. A single French woman stated:

> I know I use all my busyness to keep me from those feelings of loneliness. The irony is that I want to have an ongoing relationship, but I really have no time or energy to meet or even to go out with anyone.

Many of our efforts at staying busy, filling up our schedules and lives with people and activities, may be our way of keeping loneliness at bay, but they can also keep us from the kind of inner growth that only solitude can give us.

The opposite reaction is inactivity. Living in a foreign culture often encourages healthy introspection about our lives, but too much can lead to a mood that may intensify our feelings of isolation and loneliness. Within our homes we can create safe, familiar worlds, engaging in such solitary activities as watching TV or videos, reading, or surfing the Internet. By nurturing our loneliness, we may find ourselves retreating from people and activities.

Such a withdrawal can also be reinforced by the isolated nature of the expat community. In addition, there is the more introverted nature of Japanese society. Loneliness can then become a part of a vicious cycle or a self-fulfilling prophecy. While it is important to examine the deeper meaning of being alone, feelings of loneliness can also be a reminder that we need to spend more time in the outer world. Without the stimulation provided by people and activities, we can become ingrown, lacking the necessary spark to help ignite our inner life.

Making a Home

While there are expats with Western-style housing benefits, many must live without such privileges. This may mean, in addition to outrageous rent prices in cities, that your home may be small, noisy, dark, or inconveniently located. Also, you may have to pay a high emotional price because of possible discrimination for being non-Japanese, single, or a woman.

A primary consideration in choosing appropriate housing is location. If you work in the city, living in the suburbs, although less expensive, involves excessive commuting—leaving one exhausted or never at home. Some expats who live in bedroom communities find it annoying to have to deal with curious neighbors or unruly children. There are also fewer twenty-four-hour-type conveniences on the outskirts of towns and cities—restaurants, banks, supermarkets, dry cleaners, and such—that cater to the needs of working people. Equally important is to choose a place that is accessible to friends and colleagues. For those with children, finding a place near a school may take precedence over the needs of either parent.

In addition to location, furnishing one's home can be a challenge, considering the high cost of household goods in Japan. Fortunately, with expats coming and going, there are plenty of bargains to be found in secondhand furniture and household appliance sales. "*Sayonara* sales" advertised in local newsletters and bulletin boards provide household items at low prices or for the cost of hauling "the bargains" away.

No matter where or in what style we live, it is important to remember that our home away from home needs to be a place that is both appealing and functional. It should be an environment that can serve as a refuge from the outside world, a place to relax and unwind—a center from which to start each day.

Those who are single may not spend enough on their housing, opting for money in the bank and trips abroad. They may feel that their home is just a place to hang their hat. Not enjoying their residence, singles may spend more time outside than inside their home. Couples, with or without children, may find that living in a place smaller than is customary back home may result in a higher-than-usual level of stress and tension. Because of a lack of privacy and sense of personal space, some may "tune out," finding themselves "not at home" even at home.

Perhaps the most frustrating aspect of running a house is the Japanese assumption that there will always be someone at home to receive special deliveries, mail, or large purchases. Foreigners are especially upset by the fact that although repairmen may have promised to come, they may not show up at the agreed-upon time—or day! This has also become a source of irritation for working Japanese women who no longer have an extended family at home to take care of such matters. Many Japanese now agree that there has been a steady decline in service, so that "the customer is king" no longer. One single British woman complained:

> I went to great lengths to take the morning off from work in order to have my stove fixed. I waited all morning, but no one arrived. I called and was told that the electrician will most likely come in the afternoon. I finally got it fixed three weeks later after rearranging my schedule two times. I soon learned that "hai, hai" doesn't always mean "yes."

To help solve these and other problems, some single expats have sought roommates to help with the responsibilities of rent, household tasks, and caring for plants or pets. Although living with a virtually unknown person may pose interpersonal problems, many of these arrangements have turned out to be satisfactory, given the high cost of living in Japan and the problems posed by loneliness in general. Roommates can also give support and bring structure and balance to an expat's life through shared activities, conversing in one's own language, occasional meals together, and comfort when one is sick or feeling down.

Others have "solved" the housing problem by renting an inexpensive place in the mountains or by the seaside. To help share the costs, many have gone in with several others. It's unlikely that any one person could get away every weekend. For most people, being able to periodically get outside of one's home and leave the city can make all the difference in terms of whether one is happy living in Japan. Quite often, just knowing that you can get away is enough to help you get through the week or month. Such a second home can also be the ideal setting to invite friends and colleagues for the weekend. This is especially true for one's Japanese friends, as both the host and guest can feel comfortable in a more casual setting. In addition, getting away may mean being able to get a different glimpse of Japan and its people. Experiencing life in the countryside—rice paddies and all—may be the change of pace you've been looking for.

Friendships

Friends, or the lack of them, can make or break your stay in Japan. They should be thought of as cornerstones on which to build your life on foreign soil. In putting together your "family away from home," special care should be taken in selecting its members. Although the expat community is small, there is a variety of potential friends from which to choose. Seek friends at places of work, through clubs and associations, churches, and the many types of support and interest groups to be found in the expat and Japanese communities.

It is natural initially to seek friendships among those of your own nationality. This is especially true during the first six months, when there is a great need for familiarity and being able to communicate in one's own language. Such friends can serve as bridges between one's home country and the new culture. Long-term expats often serve as mentors, helping out in the cultural adjustment and settling-in phases.

Once you get settled, friendships with Japanese should also be considered, although they can be more difficult to make because of language and cultural differences. However, friendships with Japanese are worth pursuing because they can be vital in providing companionship and invaluable insight into the people, language, and customs of Japan. Be aware that some Japanese may feel reluctant to invest in short-term relationships.

When problems with Japanese friends do arise, they are mainly due to cultural differences. One common complaint of expats is the length of time it takes to reach a certain level of intimacy and trust. Others feel frustrated with the Japanese for being too restrained, ill-at-ease, and self-conscious or for not sharing their feelings or thoughts as readily or as openly as foreigners. Many find that a Japanese lack of casualness makes it awkward to invite friends to just "drop by" for a cup of coffee, have dinner in one's home, or take a trip together. Expat men are generally not as upset by these differences as women are, as their relationships tend to be more work- or activity-oriented—usually over a few drinks—which has a definite loosening-up effect for Japanese. As an Indonesian woman expressed it:

> The hardest thing for me was not having anyone I could talk to. Japanese are very reserved about expressing their emotions, while Indonesians aren't. I used to get so frustrated because I had to act like a Japanese, and I had nowhere to release my feelings.

The reality is that there are some Japanese who may feel equally unhappy in their interpersonal relationships. Having to be mindful of such culturally based protocols as obligation *(on)*, duty *(giri)*, and a rigid social hierarchy *(tateshakai)*, some may find it an enjoyable and enriching experience to have a relationship with a non-Japanese. If you look carefully, such friends may be found, and they may not necessarily be "returnees," or those who have also lived abroad.

Another commonly mentioned problem is how to read nonverbal cues, the most confusing being that of silence. Foreigners are often puzzled when, in the course of what seemed to be a good relationship, there is a change of personality, as shown by such behaviors as sullenness, an unwillingness to discuss a matter, or even a severing of the relationship.

For Westerners who tend to rely more on verbal communication, to be cut off in such a manner is extremely unsettling because it leaves little room for understanding, forgiveness, or reconciliation. Many Japanese, however, tend to feel that if friends are truly sensitive and caring, they should know what the transgression is without having to be told. While an ability to read each other's mind or feelings may be somewhat possible within one's own culture, it can be problematic in cross-cultural relationships.

Cross-Cultural Dating and Relationships

Becoming involved in an intimate relationship can occupy much time and energy. Even if the relationship progresses smoothly, it needs considerable care and attention. When things don't work out, one can be preoccupied with trying to figure out what went wrong, and nurturing a bruised or broken heart takes time. In some cases simply the absence of such a relationship can cause frustration. For some women it may appear that all interesting or attractive men are happily married or, if they are single, dating Japanese women. Because of an increase in the number of professional expat women in the business sector, however, the probability of meeting another expat, though not necessarily from one's own culture, is fairly high. Keep in mind that cross-cultural relationships may require extra effort by both parties.

Cultural differences that can be a source of conflict in relationships include differences in communication styles, role expectations, preconceived stereotypes, and ways of expressing affection and commitment. The fact that one partner is a "native," and thus knowledgeable of and comfortable with the local environment, while the other is a "visitor," with relatively little familiarity, can add to numerous imbalances in the relationship that can also result in conflicts. Although many cross-cultural relationships are successful, the following discussion points to some areas in which problems can arise.

A Western man who becomes involved with a Japanese woman may have a stereotypical image of his partner as being nurturing, compliant, subservient, and "feminine," in comparison to Western women. A Japanese woman, on the other hand, may have her own preconceived notions of a Western male as being more considerate, demonstrative of his feelings, assertive yet gentle, and more liberal with regard to the status of women, when compared with Japanese men.

Confusion and disappointment, even depression, may set in when the Western man realizes that in fact the Japanese woman may have many of the same negative qualities he perceived in Western women. Many men are often taken aback by the openly pursuing style of some Japanese women and by the difficulties involved in extricating oneself from the relationship, should it end. Others are left baffled when they receive the silent treatment or when the relationship ends with no warning or explanation.

Likewise, Japanese women may discover that Western men also have their own needs to be nurtured and cared for—especially in a foreign culture—even more so than the average Japanese man, who, for the most part, is rarely at home. And if one of her expectations of the relationship is to be taken away from Japan, she may feel betrayed when she learns that the Western man has no intention of returning to his home country.

Stereotypes can also play a role in relationships between Western women and Japanese men. In fact, they are often initially attracted to each other for not fitting into each other's stereotypes. Many Western women are pleasantly surprised to learn that Japanese men do not fit the stereotypical image of being withdrawn, undemonstrative, or overbearing "male chauvinists." Likewise, the Japanese man is equally surprised to learn that Western women are not really aggressive, bossy, controlling, and self-absorbed.

Often Japanese men feel trapped between a desire to please the Western woman and their need to meet the demands of society, which may include obligations to the workplace, parents, and colleagues. Western women who have met their Japanese partners overseas may find that their mate becomes a different person once back in Japan. Some couples feel that living in a third culture is less stressful for the relationship.

Generally, Western women are most bothered by the relatively small amount of time and energy that Japanese men have to give to the relationship. This may leave some women feeling suspicious or resentful of their partners' time away from them, thus eroding their sense of confidence, security, and independence. A Japanese man may then distance himself even more from the Western woman, fearing that he will never be able to fulfill her seemingly overwhelming needs. A vicious cycle can then ensue (see figure 2, p. 25).

Should the relationship lead to marriage, the same issues regarding the absent Japanese husband/father may arise. This can be especially difficult for the Western woman, who is often expected to be fully involved with Japanese society—being proficient in the Japanese language and performing many or all of the duties of a Japanese wife, daughter-in-law, and mother—all without much support from her husband. On the other hand, many women find that they have a great deal more independence and appreciate being able to develop and pursue their own interests.

Some of the concerns enumerated above may also be found in cross-cultural gay and lesbian relationships. During the past ten years, the gay community in Japan has become more visible. There has been an increase in the number of Japanese gays who have "come out" as members of the gay community. Compared with the West, however, fewer have come out to their families. This can be a source of misunderstanding and conflict for cross-cultural gay couples. When Japanese partners hide the relationship from their families, Western partners may misconstrue this as personal rejection. It is important for Westerners to understand that Japanese family dynamics may be different from what they are accustomed to. Public displays of affection among straight and gay couples are less common in Japan as than the West. Although the sight of young straight couples holding hands is not uncommon in urban areas, kissing is hardly ever observed. And such behavior is rarely seen among gay couples.

Regardless of any cross-cultural differences that may exist within gay relationships, some Westerners feel that being gay in Japan is a positive experience for them. One gay American noted:

> As an introvert I feel more comfortable in Japan as compared to back home. I certainly don't miss the political aspects of being gay in America today. I appreciate the fact that, for the most part, Japanese society respects my need for privacy—especially when it concerns something that I feel is deeply personal.

In our practice, we have found that any cross-cultural relationship in which there are similar values (see the Inventory of Personal Values, p. 81), interests, goals, a shared religious faith, and a proficiency in each other's language is more successful than one in which none or few of these characteristics exist. While this may appear to be only common sense, we have seen an increase in the number of couples who, after several years of being in a relationship, request bilingual counseling—not to be understood by the therapist but in order to be fully understood by each other.

Although cross-cultural relationships can often appear to be daunting, the reality is that all relationships have their unique set of challenges. However, an advantage for those who are in cross-cultural relationships is that they are continually reminded of this fact. Such an awareness can lead both partners never to assume what the other partner may be thinking or feeling—ultimately resulting in greater communication and appreciation of each other.

Japanese Schools and Universities

The number of families who opt to send their children to Japanese schools is growing. While a number of parents have always sent their children to Japanese preschool, many more are now sending them through the first few years of grade school. The parents' reasons for doing so may be financial considerations, lack of proximity to an international school, or wanting their children to be directly exposed to the Japanese language and culture.

Few parents express regret for sending their offspring to Japanese schools. They feel that the children not only are learning the language (especially if they are the only foreigners in the school) but are given excellent exposure to music, art, dance, and sports. Parents are also pleased that their youngsters are able to make Japanese friends. They themselves have been able to have close friendships with other parents—often with their children acting as interpreters for them. One American father remarked:

> I never thought that by putting my child in a Japanese school I would equally benefit from the experience. Not only have I had to learn my hiragana, but I have gained access to another aspect of Japanese society—something I would never have been able to do just through my contacts at work.

Language, however, can pose a problem when having to communicate with the administration or teachers, in being able to take part in PTA or parent-teacher conferences, or in helping their children with homework. Some parents are concerned about their children's national and cultural identity, differences in Japanese male/female role expectations, and whether their children will be behind in learning their own language. Still others are often taken aback when their children reject them in front of their Japanese friends for being "different."

When problems arise, it may be because of the fact that, in some instances, foreign children may get too much attention and special treatment. The Japanese teaching staff does not always place the same expectations on foreign children as they do on their Japanese students. Some parents later find that their children were not required to perform, had insufficient limits set for them, or were not disciplined. They may find their children acting more spoiled at home and lacking in basic academic and social skills.

In spite of this, for both children and parents, Japanese schooling in the formative years is a positive experience. Although children will most likely "forget" their Japanese language ability once back in their home country, the advantage is that should they ever study the language later on, they will find that their pronunciation, intonation, and nonverbal expressions will still be there for them. Usually, within three to six months after reentry, their native language control and productivity is "normal." As adults, many have found that, at the very least, they are drawn to Japan and to things Japanese.

Expat children who continue their education within the Japanese educational system may have different concerns, especially from junior high onward. Being a teenager back in one's home country or at an international school can be traumatic enough, but those who are in Japanese schools may feel even more self-conscious about their personal differences. Compared with their Japanese peers, their usually larger physical size and more mature social and sexual attitudes can lead to teasing and in some cases *ijime* (bullying), a serious problem in Japanese schools. Academically, although expat students may be ahead in such subjects as math, science, and geography, some find that their creative impulses and desires to be independent, critical thinkers have been stifled. The Japanese emphasis on rote memorization and preoccupation with multiple choice and fill-in-the-blank styles of test taking—as exemplified by the university/college entrance examinations—leaves some feeling uninspired or discouraged. In addition, expat students often cannot rely on their parents to be of help socially or academically. The issue of cultural identity will be discussed at greater length in the next chapter.

Adult foreign students, both undergraduates and graduates, may be studying in Japan anywhere from nine months to two years. Those who are not able to complete their studies or research often stay on much longer. Generally, the life of a foreign student, whether single or married, Western or non-Western, can be fairly stressful, given the fact that they are here in Japan for the purpose of fulfilling a necessary requirement for a graduate degree or research study.

Whether a student is on a scholarship or grant, with limited financial resources, the high cost of living can be a major problem—especially if one is responsible for his or her own housing. Non-Western students often complain that they are discriminated against when securing housing. Foreign students may find themselves living far from their universities to keep costs down. Those who live in dormitories may find the buildings depressing and not conducive to serious study.

Foreign students may find a lack of general support—especially those who do not have close ties with their host universities. While some may receive adequate academic, emotional, social, and housing assistance, there are those who are, for the most part, left entirely on their own. Frustration can often mount if there is dissatisfaction with the Japanese educational system. Some may complain about receiving little academic guidance from their Japanese professors, uninspired lectures and classes, and unmotivated fellow students. Even with all the extracurricular activities on and off campus, foreign students may find it difficult to be accepted by the tightly knit structures of Japanese groups and clubs, let alone to make friends.

Just by the nature of the academic community and culture in general, foreign students can often isolate themselves in their own "ivory towers." It is important for students to realize that they, too, are a part of the larger expatriate community and have a ready-made support system available to them (see Chapter 6). Those who have taken advantage of such resources have found that by having many of their emotional and social needs met in that larger community, they were better able to successfully fulfill their academic goals.

Working in Japan

Work is what brings most expats to Japan. In fact, a job can take up all of one's waking hours. To keep a balance between work, personal relationships, leisure activities, and time alone is difficult. Even if one should strive for a well-rounded lifestyle, the workaholic nature of Japanese society often does not reinforce or support our best efforts toward that goal.

Although the phenomenon of *karoshi* (death from overwork) relates primarily to Japanese men who put in long hours with little rest and poor eating and exercise habits, many Westerners are equally susceptible to overwork. Like Japan, where hard work is considered to be a virtue, the West with its notion of work and its Protestant work ethic, tends to glorify the amount of time, energy, and thought we put into our jobs. While to a certain extent our work can give us a sense of identity, self-worth, self-esteem, and direction in life, for some work may become an end in itself.

There are now health professionals in the West who believe that "workaholism" is just as serious as any other addiction. Researchers have noted that sufferers experience withdrawal symptoms when not working—work being an activity that can produce a mental, emotional, or even physical high due to an "adrenaline rush" brought on by pushing oneself too hard. Like any addiction, most workaholics will deny or rationalize to themselves and others why they must work so hard.

Some of the signs to be aware of in identifying whether one is heading in an unhealthy direction include the following: a general tendency toward busyness, rushing, or rescuing—usually accompanied by being late or missing appointments and deadlines; saying yes to most requests; feeling that only we can get the job done; an obsessive-compulsive, driven quality in what one thinks and does; long work hours with little time off; and lack of proper sleep. Often, time off means a "working vacation" when one may even feel anxious being separated from the workplace. Voice and e-mail, faxes, and cellular phones can keep one feeling "connected" at any time and in any place. In one's social life, spending time with family and friends becomes less satisfying than that of enhancing work-related relationships. Healthwise, one may suffer from headaches, backaches, insomnia, high blood pressure, and depression. To compound the problem, workaholism often goes unrecognized and thus untreated, as Western (particularly American) society generally rewards those who are "successful," whether it be in accruing wealth, status, accomplishments, or "good works."[1]

As most expats in Japan are "successful," or at the very least highly motivated—enough to leave their home countries—the tendency toward overwork is high. It therefore behooves us to first recognize where we are on the work/overwork continuum. Only then can we honestly answer whether working in Japan has been responsible for turning us into "workaholics" (as many complain) or whether Japan has only reinforced or accentuated preexisting tendencies.

In addition to the personal work styles and habits we may have brought with us from our home countries, difficulties may also arise that are unique to the Japanese work situation. A major dissatisfaction for some expats working in office settings (often smoke-filled) are the long hours—even though one has already satisfactorily accomplished his or her responsibilities. In fact, to do one's work quickly and accurately in Japan may mean having to figure out how to expand work in order to fill the leftover time—not an easy feat with office mates all around you. Activities like frequent meetings, after-hours socializing, golf games, and company trips can seem a waste of time when expats want more time for their families, friends, and personal interests—evenings, weekends, and holidays. With time on one's hands, it is not uncommon to feel bored, restless, and unmotivated. The Japanese notion of group cohesiveness and teamwork-building is a bitter pill to swallow for those expats raised on the values of individual talent and achievement, which reward efficiency and productivity in the workplace.

A common work-related problem experienced by expats is the disparity between what one thought he or she was going to do and what one actually does on the job. Many expats have come to Japan not only for the opportunity, pay, and experience but for the challenge and responsibility they thought a job would bring. Instead, they may find that their jobs offer very little room or opportunity for creativity, taking the initiative, or providing leadership. In many cases, one's education, training, and experience will not seem to have any relationship to what one is doing. Under these circumstances, expats may feel frustrated, stifled, misused, and unappreciated. They may often learn that following routines and procedures and the need to suppress themselves for the group and company is not their style. As a result, expats may be forced to decide between financial stability and finding more fulfilling work.

In particular, making suggestions for a new product or implementing a new idea may not be all that well received. Most often one's Japanese boss and colleagues will say that an idea or product is not viable, or simply state, *"Dekimasen"* (it can't be done). After being told this more than once, it does not take long for the expat to realize that even if the idea is a good one, by the time it receives approval from everyone concerned, one has either lost interest or has moved on to something different. Such a seemingly "negative" reaction to try anything new goes against the more innovative, risk-taking nature of many non-Japanese. For the Japanese, a more "cautious," conservative approach to trying anything new is believed to make good business sense, and failure is to be avoided at all costs.

Still another commonly expressed dissatisfaction is the lack of feedback—good or bad—about one's performance. Most Westerners want and need some kind of tangible evidence or verbal acknowledgment that they are on the right track—especially in a new culture. Many feel that they are forced to function in a vacuum and must second-guess what is expected of them.

Even the most confident, highly trained expat can eventually feel unglued, unappreciated, or incompetent. Added to this is the fact that expats may also have lost the ability, sensitivity, or desire—possibly from feeling undernourished themselves—to offer feedback to their friends and colleagues.

Some Japanese bosses withhold positive feedback for fear that employees will ask for an increase in pay or responsibilities. They may also not wish to be seen as giving special preference to certain individuals, or they may believe that giving praise will actually lead to a drop in overall performance. There are also bosses who may choose to exert their influence or, as a result of insecurity, may even question or criticize a native speaker's language ability, while having little or no knowledge of the language themselves. Unfortunately, many Japanese bosses do not realize that withholding positive feedback, and in some cases giving only negative feedback, does not increase employee productivity or help foster company spirit. Instead, it may be a sure way to lose an otherwise enthusiastic and productive expat employee.

In addition to experiencing the dissatisfactions mentioned above, some expats may find that their Japanese bosses do not take their complaints seriously enough, particularly when dealing with the issue of workplace harassment. Offending behaviors may range from verbal and emotional abuse to sexual harassment. Many expats are often left feeling unsupported when their boss does not show concern or take action. They may be told that it is up to them to improve the situation. There is a tendency for Japanese to stay out of other people's business if it is perceived as something "personal." As Japanese are generally reluctant to confront and are equally uncomfortable in dealing with disharmony or discord, they may ignore the problem or hope that it will go away on its own. Thus, very few employees are reprimanded, disciplined, or fired for inappropriate interpersonal workplace behavior. Many expats, finding the workplace too uncomfortable, search for a more hospitable work environment and, in a few cases, return to their home country.

Although the Japanese workplace can be fraught with difficulties, one Australian man remarked:

> There have been many times I wanted to quit my job and go back home. However, whenever I got to this point I would remind myself that things aren't really any worse in Japan—just different.

4 Staying On

One's homeland is wherever one does well.
—Cicero
Roman philosopher

A sizable number of expatriates find themselves living and working in Japan beyond their first assignment or intended time of stay, or return to Japan after completing their initial sojourn. A significant number of foreigners have, from the outset, made long-term commitments to stay in Japan. Regardless of how and why some find themselves staying on, statistics show that the number of foreign nationals who do continues to rise each year. Long-term residents are mainly those who are in business, education, or religious work, with their families or with spouses of Japanese nationality.

Adult Long-Term Residents

As we explore some of the issues encountered by long-term residents, keep in mind that for the most part this group of expatriates is living and working in Japan by choice. Generally, the decision to stay on is made after weighing many of the advantages and disadvantages of life here and after considering the changing economic, social, cultural, and political situations in their home countries. When problems do arise, they tend to fall into one of the following broad categories.

Living in Limbo Although embassies, church mission boards, educational institutions, military organizations, and many of the larger businesses send their employees to Japan for a specified number of years, some expats find themselves in the unsettling situation of having an open-ended time frame for their stay.

This happens most frequently to the businessman and his family who are asked to extend their stay in Japan beyond the initially agreed-upon time period. What began as a three-year commitment becomes a five- to eight-year sojourn, which significantly affects the family's ability to make plans for the future.

Uncertainty then may become a way of life. The husband is often better able to cope with this situation, because it is a part of his job, but the wife may suffer by having to put her own personal and professional life on hold. Some wives feel frustrated, angry, or depressed, and very much out of control of their lives and bereft of their ability to influence or make plans for the present or future. When living in limbo, ordinary questions become uncommonly difficult to answer, such as the following: Should I take the necessary next step in seriously learning the language? Should I take on a responsible commitment or start a part- or full-time job? Should I look for more permanent housing?

Another group of expatriates who find themselves in limbo are those who came to Japan with the intent of staying only one or two years but end up staying five, ten, or more years. Some were initially just passing through and decided to stay, while others had finished their college degree and wanted to take some time out before deciding what to do next. Still others have successfully completed a one-to-three-year private or government-sponsored teaching contract and now wish to continue their graduate studies. Working primarily as English teachers or doing other freelance work, some of these residents have accomplished their initial goals of obtaining work experience (although frequently not in their field of training or interest), saving money, learning about Japanese culture, and seeing the rest of Asia.

Those who find themselves in this situation often feel an inner unrest, a nagging feeling that it is time to move on, but they find it difficult to do so. Issues centered on unresolved conflicts with parents, marital status, career goals, and the need to learn the language or receive further education or training begin to surface. This state of limbo is most acute during visa-renewal time—an unwelcome reminder that time is moving on and that a decision either to remain in Japan (on a more or less permanent basis) or to return home has not yet been made.

Typical of those in this situation is an American in his late twenties who had been teaching English here for six years:

> Sometimes living and working in Japan feels like a cop-out. My parents and friends think I'm doing something really important here—if they only knew the truth. I know I can't go on like this for too much longer. It makes me too anxious.

High Cost of Living Everyone suffers from the high cost of living in Japan, but those who are committed to staying for an indefinite period of time usually suffer the most. The higher living costs are more keenly felt by those who once had a full expatriate package—subsidized housing, club memberships, home leaves, tuition expenses, a cost-of-living allowance, etc.—but lost those benefits after becoming a "local hire." They then find themselves living on the Japanese economy, sometimes in straitened financial circumstances.

In making long-range plans, the long-term resident must also consider the financial impact of the potential loss of home-country Social Security or welfare benefits. Even after a lengthy employment in Japan, the long-term resident may be unable to get such benefits in Japan.

While short-termers may be able to live with exorbitant rent prices and the lack of adequate space for a limited amount of time, those who stay on must consider the long-term costs of housing in Japan. Many long-termers resent giving up a sizable portion of their income for rent. Without permanent-resident visa status, bank mortgages are difficult to come by in Japan. Those who are able to buy a home must often live outside of major cities, far from their place of work or their children's school.

The stress brought on by Japan's high cost of living is acutely felt within the marital relationship. The wife may feel cheated, while the husband may feel he is an inadequate provider for his family. Raising a family is no longer a natural part of married life, but rather a luxury, especially in view of the high costs of annual tuition to an international school (while at the same time the family might be saving for their child's college education). Even if a family is able to afford the tuition at an international school, teenagers may feel left out and continually frustrated, being unable to socially compete with their peers who have access to the American Club, live in Homat homes, or spend their winter holidays skiing in Switzerland. Such unhappiness for teens, who desire more than anything to be like everyone else, may be expressed directly to parents by sullen or moody behaviors.

High Rate of Community Turnover Having gone through the honeymoon period and experienced culture shock and the period of cultural adjustment (refer to the U-Curve, Chapter 2), long-term expatriates may soon find themselves in the position of watching other people come and go. After saying farewell to two or three friends as they return home or move on to other assignments, some expats realize that they are caught up in performing an unsatisfying role, which may be limiting personal growth or leading to burnout.

It is a common scenario. The long-term resident meets the new expatriate, and during the newcomer's honeymoon phase a friendship develops based on common interests or background. The newcomer relies on the new friend's knowledge and experience through the critical culture-shock period and through the period of cultural adjustment because, after all, the friend is an old hand in Japan. During this first year, the long-term resident assumes the role of mentor, guide, and information bank. Just as the relationship has become a truly two-way street—that is, conversation no longer centers on living in Japan or the expatriate life—the long-term resident must then live through the newfound friend's preparations to leave Japan.

For those left behind, letting go of personal relationships in which one has invested so much energy and time can be traumatic. Even if friendships continue through correspondence, long-term residents often find themselves fulfilling the role of foreign correspondent, keeping Japan alive for absent friends. If aware of this phenomenon, short-term residents can become more sensitive to the reluctance many long-term residents have about starting new relationships.

When several friends leave at once, expatriates must deal with feelings of loss, which may become overwhelming if the loss is coupled with the death of a parent or friend in the home country. Dealing with a loss back home forces one to reevaluate the notion that even while friends continually come and go in Japan, things will remain stable back home.

Professionally, it may become tiresome for long-term expats to sit on committees or boards or to be in work situations where they must deal with highly motivated directors or chairpersons—usually in their honeymoon phase—who bring from their home countries "new ideas" and the "latest ways" of doing things. As a result, some long-termers grow weary of "reinventing the wheel" every few years, knowing what does and doesn't work in situations in Japan. Like friendships, just when work relationships become a two-way street—usually after newcomers have adjusted their expectations to reality—their time is up, once again, leaving the long-termer holding the bag. It helps if short-termers can understand why some long-termers avoid being overly involved in even well-meaning causes or refuse invitations to speak to groups about various aspects of living in Japan.

The long-term resident is confronted with the basic problem of dealing with a continually changing support network. The problem is compounded by the fact that the long-term resident is often isolated from other long-term residents. Japan does not have a distinct population or tradition of an established network of long-term expatriates, as is found in India or Singapore. If there is an ongoing support network, it is usually based on shared professional interests or nationality, rather than encompassing the whole group of long-term expatriates.

Career Changes

> I know I will have to go to the States to get my M.A. degree if I hope to get anywhere in my field. Somehow I feel that living in Japan has limited my options. After all, I couldn't just leave my husband and children, even if it was just for a few months.
>
> —American woman married to a Japanese citizen

By and large, long-term residents have chosen to live in Japan because of economically or emotionally satisfying work conditions. However, the spouses of long-term residents or the parties of a divorce or a death in the family often feel that their career options are limited or unfulfilling. In these circumstances, career counseling can be a valuable service.

Career counseling helps one explore his or her own readiness to pursue a career and to learn where abilities and talents lie. Career changes can also be explored; for example, is there life after teaching English? Finding appropriate and affordable institutions for training or further education in one's field of choice and native language is frequently the next problem the Japan resident will face.

An increasing number of expats are taking advantage of the many correspondence courses offered to those living overseas and the extension programs that are located in Japan, in order to obtain an academic degree. Before enrolling, always contact a well-established college or university in your home country and ask whether it would accept credits or a degree from the institution in question. Keep in mind, when considering further training or education, that knowing the Japanese language is equivalent to, if not more marketable than, most academic degrees when your work involves Japan. One need not look too far for examples of expats who have carved out successful careers for themselves both in Japan and back home, where knowing the language gives them the competitive edge.

Becoming Part of the Culture Both short- and long-term residents should give some thought to the extent with which they will become involved with the host culture. It's an individual matter, and the degree of assimilation can usually be determined by the expatriate. This is especially true for individuals living in the larger cities, where a comfortable balance between the expatriate and Japanese communities is more easily found. For those living in smaller cities or rural areas, assimilation may not be an option but a necessity.

The long-term residents most affected by the assimilation question are those in cross-cultural marriages. This is true for both urban and non-urban residents. For these individuals, there is little choice regarding the degree of assimilation because they must meet the expectations of spouses, in-laws, friends, and work colleagues. If they have children in the Japanese school system, non-Japanese spouses may have the additional burden of meeting both the children's needs as well as the expectations of those involved in their offspring's school life, i.e., other parents, students, and teachers.

The "go native" group, whose goal is specifically to become a part of Japanese society, has similar difficulties. The members of this group are usually long-term residents involved in mastering one of the traditional Japanese arts. They will have invested a great deal of time and energy in the assimilation process and may feel their efforts are unrewarded.

Those attempting some degree of assimilation can feel bitter and hurt at times and ask themselves, What am I doing wrong? or, What more can I do? They must come to terms with the fact that language proficiency, knowledge, sensitivity to the culture, or the number of years already spent in Japan are not necessarily prerequisites for successful assimilation. Those who, like many others, resent being called *gaijin* (foreigner) or even *gaikokujin* (foreign national) should keep in mind that many Japanese are also *yosomono* (strangers or outsiders) when they live in a place other than their birthplace. For example, as young people have increasingly moved from the *furusato* (hometown) to urban areas for education, career, and marriage purposes, they are often considered as *yosomono* by their neighbors.

Coping with this situation means accepting who you are and striving to achieve a balance in integrating the Japanese culture with your own. Enjoy being the honored guest—the *gaijin*—and take pleasure in the positive feedback the Japanese accord dedicated students of Japan.

Surviving Life Stages Growth does not stop upon reaching adulthood. Studies show that an adult can suffer from "growth pains" more painful than those experienced in adolescence. The long-term expatriate must, like anyone else, pass through the necessary life stages—but there are some differences.

Going through life's normal changes that occur as a result of marriage, the birth and raising of children, the empty-nest syndrome, beginning and changing employment, midlife crisis, menopause, retirement, and dealing with illness or death do not go unnoticed within the expatriate and Japanese communities. For those who value their privacy, this public visibility can add even more strain to what are already stressful situations. Long-term residents are often known in their respective communities for being "successful" or for "always having it together." Recognizing and dealing with these normal growth problems for themselves or others can be difficult when even having a problem is seen as weakness.

Individuals often find that they need a safe place to deal with the stressful life-stage problems with which they are confronted. They may feel reluctant to talk to friends and colleagues for fear of a lack of confidentiality. All this contributes to their sense of isolation regarding their predicament.

In contrast to what might be available in the home country, expats may find a lack of wider community support, such as support groups and workshops dealing with specific life-stage problems, as well as an overall lack of information from books, lectures, special television programs, etc. For many, just having a "reality check" and knowing that this is a normal, predictable life stage is very reassuring.

Geographical Isolation Not all long-term expatriates live within the confines of larger cities where sizable expatriate communities, international schools, places of worship with services conducted in one's own language, medical facilities where English is spoken, and support groups, clubs, and English-language bookstores can be found. In fact, many live on the outskirts of large cities or in midsize cities in country areas because housing costs are lower (either renting or owning) or because their employment brings them there.

While the breadwinner commutes daily or returns home a few days a week, the spouse may be left behind with young children. In many cases, a weekly trip into the city is the only chance these individuals have to visit a friend and speak their native language, to stock up on unavailable goods, or to attend a lecture, class, or meeting. These expatriates often confront loneliness and feelings of general alienation from both the Japanese and foreign communities. Many who find themselves in this situation are forced to plan for their children's education and their own work and continuing education while isolated from the very resources necessary to make these decisions.

Caring for Aging or Ill Relatives The issue of how best to care for ill or aging relatives is a universal concern, but those living and working outside their home country are presented with additional difficulties. On a visit home, the expatriate may be required to make on-the-spot decisions about things like hospitalization, the type of care (retirement home versus state facility), insurance, pension plans, and wills. These sudden decisions are frequently made without adequate preparation and in the absence of current information regarding laws, options, or entitlement programs.

Responding to the needs of relatives back home, especially in a crisis, often raises feelings of guilt about having chosen or accepted an overseas assignment. The expatriate is confronted with issues dealing with duty and responsibility to, or general estrangement from, the family. For long-term expatriates approaching retirement, this can bring up the painful issue of how they will be cared for if they are confronted with a debilitating illness or injury in their old age.

Children of Long-Term Residents

Most parents living in their home country who are trying to raise physically and emotionally healthy children have support networks and an abundance of professional guides equivalent to Dr. Spock. Expats who are trying to accomplish a similar feat in Japan are often left with an uneasy feeling concerning how their children will eventually "turn out" as a result of an extended overseas experience. For these parents, it is not uncommon to harbor the following fears: Will my child grow up rootless, without a real sense of personal or cultural identity? Is it harmful to my child's linguistic ability to mix Japanese and English words in one sentence? What effect does it have on my child to go back and forth between Japan and our home country, and to constantly cope with two cultures, new schools, and new friends?

One well-known team of sociologists, Dr. Ruth Hill Useem and Dr. John Useem, coined the term *third culture* to describe the ever-changing environment in which overseas children are reared. They defined "third-culture kids" (TCKs) as dependents of parents who are employed abroad and who feel most at home in a third culture "which is created, shared, and carried by persons who are relating societies, or sections thereof, to each other." This third culture is not the fusion or accommodation of one's home culture or nationality with that of a second or host culture; rather it is a culture in and of itself, with its own set of values, expectations, styles of living, and identities.[1] In contrast to the view that children who are products of two (or more) cultures are considered to be "marginal," that is, unable to identify with either culture and forever lost between the two, the concept of TCKs approaches the matter on a more positive note.

The offspring of cross-cultural marriages are generally thought of as bicultural, binational, or, more recently, people with dual nationality. These terms can apply to children raised within the context of Japanese society who go through the Japanese educational system and later choose Japan as their primary country of employment and residence. On the other hand, children who are products of cross-cultural marriages may feel more comfortable in being thought of as TCKs because they have attended international schools, either in Japan or abroad. They may have difficulty deciding which culture they feel most "at home" in and, later, as adults, can feel conflicted about where to live and work. Fortunately, as Japan has become more open-minded and accepting of bicultural children, many have been able to find a niche for themselves in Japanese society. Where once they may have felt unwelcomed, bicultural persons are increasingly receiving the respect of the Japanese people.

Each child's experience of growing up in Japan is unique, and the way children choose to define themselves is ultimately a personal decision, including the option of not being labeled at all. Regardless of preference, children raised in a bicultural environment must feel part of something larger than themselves and their immediate families.

From all indications, it does not appear that TCKs have more problems than non-TCKs. This observation not only derives from our own personal and professional experience but also correlates with studies conducted by the Useems and other researchers who have studied the social and psychological adjustments of TCKs.[2] Also substantiating this view is Ray F. Downs, a long-time headmaster of the American School in Japan, who, over almost three decades, has had the unique opportunity not only of being a third-culture person himself but of observing a significant number of TCKs, from more than forty nationalities.[3]

When problems do arise, they tend to fall into one or more of the categories discussed below. Although the problems presented here are specifically related to TCKs who are dependents of long-term residents, short-termers, depending on the intensity of a family's involvement with the Japanese culture, can also have TCKs. Many of the problems confronting TCKs are similar to those confronted by children of the "privileged" or "elite" classes in Europe or the United States, although the TCK may not enjoy the same economic or social status.

Separation from Parents One general characteristic attributed to TCKs is that, as a group, they are emotionally closer to their parents than are non-TCKs. When families must live in a culture other than their own, the family unit becomes a culture in itself, representing not only one's individual identity as a member of a family with an expatriate history but also one's identity as a member of a particular nation, religious faith, occupational group, etc.—each with its own set of values, language, rules of conduct, and expectations.

For the child raised overseas, the nuclear family unit is the only source of continuity within an ever-changing environment—new cultures, schools, and friends, and sporadic contact with other families and relatives back home. The family learns how to cope together, each in its own individual fashion, in order to deal with each new situation. Over the years this experience leads to the creation of a family system in which both the parents and children become emotionally interdependent on one another and in which each member plays a vital role in handling the stresses of adjusting to living overseas. Often parent-child boundaries are blurred as the TCKs, having learned the language and unspoken rules of a given culture more quickly than their parents, find themselves assuming adult-like roles by becoming the cultural mediator between their families and the host culture.

> I soon learned that "parents" is a dirty word. My friends think I'm weird for wanting to go back to Japan for Thanksgiving, Christmas, and summer vacation. It seems as if that's the last thing anybody would want to do. For me, being with my parents has a lot to do with living in Japan. The two seem to go together somehow.
> —Third-year college student

Given the close-knit nature of the long-term expatriate family, it is understandable that separating emotionally from one's parents can be a lifelong task. This is particularly true for TCKs raised in Japan, a culture that reinforces close family ties with respect to choice of schools, employment, marriage partner, and place of residence. Although TCKs raised in Japan may not consciously take their parents' feelings into consideration when making an important decision, unconsciously there is a tendency to seek the parents' support if not outright approval of their own actions. TCKs may view parents not as authority figures from whom they need to obtain permission, but rather as companions with whom they have shared many intense life experiences.

Separating from parents to go to college is often the most traumatic time for TCKs, particularly if they must return to a culture with which they are unfamiliar. As part of the normal separation process, TCKs may rebel most effectively (if they do at all) by attacking the occupation of their parents—the very thing that identifies most expatriates.

Even if TCKs successfully manage to separate from their parents in order to attend college, a strong desire to rejoin the nuclear family may still exist. Some parents may find themselves dealing with the "full-nest syndrome" in which children return to Japan and to their parents, expecting to continue the expatriate lifestyle, much as before. For some TCKs, trying to duplicate their parents' lifestyle, to which they have grown accustomed, becomes a challenge. At the same time, parents may consciously or unconsciously find it difficult to let go of their children, equally desiring to maintain the structure, function, and unique experiences of the expatriate family situation.

Parental and Community Expectations TCKs growing up in Japan learn from an early age that much is expected of them. In many cases, parents here have a sponsoring organization, and TCKs must meet the standards of the company, mission board, or embassy, as well as be a representative of a particular nation, religious group, and set of parents. Any serious misconduct by a TCK is an embarrassment for the two countries involved. TCKs grow up well aware of what is required of them and of the impact their actions can have on their parents. The rules of the sponsor and the host culture are quite clear.

On a more individual level, the TCK must also meet the demands of parents and schools. Not only does the Japanese culture reinforce the value of education, but the expatriate community also has its own standard of academic excellence. Since there is no public school system for the expatriate community, TCKs attend either an international or a Japanese school. Because of language considerations and long-range educational goals, many opt for an international school, which is, in effect, a college preparatory school, where a majority of the students continue on to university. This presents a special problem for TCKs who are not academically oriented or skilled.

In addition to the explicit demands of the host culture, parents, the parents' sponsor, the expatriate community, and the international or Japanese school, TCKs must meet another unspoken demand. They are also expected to be 100 percent knowledgeable about both their own culture and the host culture—in other words, 200 percent culturally informed. This is particularly true regarding language ability, an impossible task for two reasons. First, it is almost impossible for a non-native speaker to achieve a level of total language mastery. Second, individuals who have not spent their entire lives in the host culture do not have access to all the necessary background and cultural history upon which humor, idioms, obscenities, clichés, and irony are based, enriching the language. TCKs may become overly self-conscious about what they perceive as a personal deficiency, not recognizing the inherent limitations of being a non-native speaker.

Constant Change As previously mentioned, for short- or long-term adult expatriates and their dependents, change—with the accompanying issues of separation and loss—is a major part of life in Japan. For TCKs, constant change presents special problems, especially when it is brought on by factors beyond their control, with little preparation or advance notice, and complicated by belated or inadequate emotional or parental support.

Some believe that frequent change during the formative childhood years better equips children for what they will face in the adult world. While that may be true, and many TCKs often grow up to be adaptable, flexible, sensitive, and seekers of new challenges, it is also true that one's strengths are sometimes one's weaknesses.

At an early age, the TCK's change antennae are particularly sensitive, on the lookout for situations that involve some sort of life alteration. Such sensitivity can have two divergent results. Some TCKs may, at some point in their lives, become fearful of change, desiring only to put down roots, while others go to the opposite extreme and are able to make many changes but are unable to make lasting commitments to higher educational goals, careers, friendships, or marriage partners. These TCKs need to look at their more vulnerable feelings of fear, sadness, loneliness, and helplessness. These feelings may never have been allowed full expression because of the pressure of meeting the expectations of others along with their own. Even TCKs who are somewhere in the middle of these two extremes, but who find themselves living overseas, may have serious reservations about starting a family, knowing all too well what could be in store for them and their children.

Being Special TCKs must deal with the special status accorded to *gaijin*, regardless of their age, length of time in Japan, and social or work status. Some TCKs exploit this special status; most do not. Initially granted certain favors and concessions by the Japanese by virtue of being foreigners, TCKs continue to enjoy such treatment over long periods of time because, having learned the language, they are able to effectively communicate their desires and intentions on an appropriate emotional and cultural level. Basic concepts like *on* (obligation) and *giri* (duty) become second nature to the personality of the TCK raised in Japan.

Many parents worry unnecessarily that the special *gaijin* status will hurt their children's growth and development. While at times it can have negative effects, it is surprising how little being special "spoils" the TCK. Because of such nurturing factors as intact families, domestic help, and a sense of local neighborhood and because of the generally positive view that Japanese society has of children, the TCK is able to grow in an environment in which most emotional and physical needs are met at the proper time of development, especially during the critical years from birth to four years of age. To a surprising degree, Japan has proved to be an ideal country in which to raise young children.

Academic "specialness" may be problematic for many TCKs. Some students whose grades averaged B or lower while attending college-prep schools in Japan find themselves at the top of their class when they return home. Since this group gained their increased academic success at a later point in their lives (usually in college), they have the feeling that somehow they may not have really earned their accomplishments. No matter what they accomplish, there is a vague sense of unreality and unworthiness about their "good fortune." These TCKs may suffer from the common "fear-of-success syndrome" or the more popularized "imposter syndrome." They share a disbelief and feeling of guilt about being able to have their desires, whether it be a scholarship, social recognition, a good job, or residence in a country of their choice. If anything, having too many options can be just as distressing as having too few.

It seems that no matter where they turn, whether in their home country or a foreign land, TCKs are either special, unusual, or an object of attention. Some TCKs choose to work at being "ordinary" by playing down their background and avoiding the limelight. Those who find this specialness a problem have an intense desire to be left alone and often wish to attend large universities where they can get lost in the crowd. They may resent the attention that was showered upon them, once as children and now as adults.

> One of the reasons I came to the States was just to get away from it all—to be like anyone else. The problem was just that when I said I grew up in Japan, everyone made a big deal of it, like asking me stupid questions or saying "what an interesting life" I must have had. Soon I stopped talking about where I came from. The attention I get here feels worse in some ways than the kind I got in Japan.
> —Second-year college student

Many who have similar feelings "drop out" of specialness status (especially being academically successful) and strive to lead what they consider to be ordinary lives. This laid-back approach can become a problem for significant others—parents, teachers, employers, spouses—who may feel that the TCK is not taking full advantage of his or her unique background and should be doing something more with his or her life.

Lack of Street Smarts Close family ties and long school hours combine to give TCKs a certain sophistication in academic and cultural matters. But they may lack exposure to the brand of practical knowledge known as "street smarts," ranging anywhere from the mechanical and social aspects of driving a car to being able to identify and deal with con artists.

The problem is compounded by the fact that in Japan, one of the safest countries in the world in which to live, it is difficult for parents to teach their children to beware of the potential hazards of the city streets back home because there are relatively few examples to draw upon. Even when there is the occasional theft or automobile accident, the efficiency and concern of the Japanese police, especially toward *gaijin*, is so reassuring that TCKs feel no need to raise their guard. In short, the TCK has not been raised in an environment of fear, and thus implicitly trusts what is in the world.

This lack of street smarts is a definite handicap when TCKs return to their home countries for the first extended stay, for example, to attend college. Unfortunately, it often takes a few bad experiences before TCKs are convinced that not everyone can be trusted and that one must look out for one's own best interests. Homecoming can be a very rude awakening for TCKs who may have idealized their home country.

The task then is to balance those qualities of openness, trustfulness, and nonaggressiveness with an appropriate amount of caution. Some find that support groups or a course in assertiveness training in their home country is an effective way to learn the ins and outs of their temporarily unfamiliar culture.

Playing the Mediating Role For TCKs who have grown up in more than one culture, taking on the mediating role is second nature to them. They often find themselves playing the role of peacemakers, negotiators, arbitrators, liaisons, and go-betweens. The mediating role for a child may have once been a satisfactory one, but as adults, some find themselves experiencing symptoms of stress or burnout, or feeling used or abused. There is a tendency to feel overly responsible for the welfare of both sides, intuitively understanding all too well each party's needs, desires, and viewpoints. Some may feel unappreciated, especially "local hires," who are generally underpaid in comparison with their colleagues, who may have neither language ability nor cultural sensitivity. As one TCK aptly put it, "It's great to be a bridge, but bridges get walked over." This sentiment is echoed by a TCK businesswoman who represents a foreign company in Japan:

> I can never seem to win. If business negotiations don't go well, I get blamed by both sides. If they go smoothly, then they believe they can do without me. One way or another I feel as if I'm always fighting for my job.

Some TCKs have little awareness or confidence in their skills and talents as mediators. Since mediating is an ability acquired through experience, TCKs can often sell themselves short, and employers can take them for granted, neither side realizing that the TCK is doing tasks that would normally take several people to perform.

5 Coping

All living souls welcome whatsoever they are ready to cope with; all else they ignore, or pronounce to be monstrous and wrong, or deny to be possible.
—George Santayana
American philosopher

Coping is the way in which an individual draws on personal, social, and psychological resources to protect oneself from stressful life experiences. Social resources consist of interpersonal networks, such as family, friends, colleagues, neighbors, and other support groups, while psychological resources are inner resources, such as personal strengths and one's outlook on life. Given that all of us encounter a myriad of stressful events in any given day, ranging from rush-hour traffic and deadlines to making important business or life decisions, coping is part of everyone's daily activity.

Most people are adept at coping and dealing with daily strains, yet the complexities of living in a new culture often require them to develop or acquire new coping skills. There is no single or ideal way to cope with the pressure of living in a foreign culture. Unfortunately, there is no magic wand that can allay all the difficulties and hardships in one stroke. However, research indicates that the most effective copers are individuals who have developed a wide repertoire of coping mechanisms.[1]

There are generally three approaches to coping with stressful situations. One is to change the situation that is causing the stress, another is to change your attitude toward the stressful situation, and the third is to accommodate to the stress.

For example, if the inability to speak Japanese is creating a considerable amount of stress for you, you have the following three choices: (1) change the situation by either trying to make the Japanese speak your language (a highly unrealistic endeavor) or becoming adept at Japanese yourself; (2) change your attitude by reassuring yourself that you're not the only *gaijin* who does not speak Japanese and that there are, after all, plenty of Japanese who do speak your own language; and (3) accommodate to the stress by avoiding situations in which you will be forced to converse in Japanese, limiting your social environment to people who speak the same language as you do, or accepting and living with the difficulties that are imposed by not understanding the language.

Because there is no one correct way to cope, you must decide upon the best alternative for yourself in any given situation. But there are some commonly agreed-upon methods for coping with specific problems. For example, in a marital situation, it is more effective to voice your dissatisfaction and try to improve the relationship. It is important for parents to take an active role in exerting influence over their children rather than passively accepting and giving in to their children's problematic behaviors. Adjusting your goals by lowering the importance attached to monetary success is said to be one of the most effective ways to cope with stresses related to economic matters.[2]

The first step in coping with the pressure of living in Japan is to become aware of what is stressful. It is only after recognizing what brings about the stress that you can mobilize your resources to effect change, either by changing the situation or changing your attitude about it.

The following are five aspects of the coping process. None of them stand alone; they are all interrelated and are integral to the total coping experience.

Becoming Aware of Your Feelings and Reactions

A fundamental key to coping lies in being in touch with your feelings and reactions. Emotional, "gut level," and physical reactions are important in that they serve as antennae to alert you that something is out of kilter. This may sound simple, but it is often difficult for any of us to be aware of what we are experiencing on a gut level. There are several reasons for this. First, we have a tendency to ignore negative feelings, figuring they will eventually disappear if we sweep them under the rug. Second, we tend to be hard on ourselves by believing that to feel weary, sad, or homesick means we are indulging in self-pity. Third, some of us are unaware of the different feelings we may be experiencing, and we simplify our reactions by categorizing them into "feeling good," "feeling so-so," or "feeling low." One American woman stated:

> I knew I was feeling depressed when things weren't going well. My oldest daughter hated her international school, all my kids missed their old neighborhood, my husband was stressed-out from work, and I was feeling awful. I couldn't discipline my kids anymore. I was gaining weight and I didn't feel like socializing. Then I realized that I was feeling too responsible for the whole thing and that's why I was feeling depressed. I had thought it was all my fault. I was the one who wanted an overseas assignment. I thought it would be a great experience for the whole family. But we came, and everyone seemed so miserable, and I felt responsible for the whole thing. But then I realized this was silly. It wasn't all my responsibility. My husband did agree that it would be a good idea, and he's the one who got the job to work in Japan. After that I felt much better and I had so much more energy.

By becoming aware that she was feeling too responsible, this woman was then able to see things from a clearer perspective. She began to feel less guilty and less depressed. This enabled her to take a firmer stand toward her children. She remained empathetic to their feelings, but she no longer gave in to their excuses for not doing things because they were feeling miserable. She was able to mobilize her inner resources as she had in the United States and thereby helped her family see the positive aspects of moving to Japan.

In the process of coping, it is necessary to identify and examine what you feel so you can act on those feelings that may be immobilizing you. The Emotional Inventory on page 79 lists a variety of emotions. Go through the list and check the feelings or reactions you may be experiencing. In reviewing what you have checked, take note also of your answers to the following questions and add the results to what you have learned about your feelings:

> How long have you had these feelings—for years, months, weeks, days, or hours?
> What is the intensity of the feelings—are they mild, moderate, intense?

Do you recognize seemingly contradictory feelings experienced at the same time, e.g., love and hatefulness?

Have you experienced any new feelings since your arrival in Japan, such as a sense of being cut off from others or feeling wishy-washy?

Have you experienced any of the old feelings from childhood or adolescence, such as awkwardness or helplessness?

Accepting Your Feelings and Reactions

While some of us are good at recognizing our reactions, others have difficulty accepting them. Certain feelings are uncomfortable to acknowledge. Some of us may have been trained at an early age to ignore certain feelings that connote weakness, such as loneliness, despair, and fear. Many individuals tend to be hard on themselves, unable to accept, for example, feeling lonely. Some carry about figurative rubber mallets, beating themselves whenever they feel weak and telling themselves that they should not be experiencing such feelings. This is especially true for those brought up in a Western culture.

When these feelings are ignored and held inside, they can manifest themselves in physical symptoms. The body rebels. This is frequently seen among men. Cardiovascular problems, susceptibility to colds, and constant fatigue are the warning signals the body uses to tell us that we are not taking care of our emotional needs.

The ways in which individuals cope psychologically with unwanted or unpleasant feelings or situations are known in the psychoanalytic field as defense mechanisms. Defense mechanisms are unconscious coping methods, and individuals are rarely aware of using them.

Some defense mechanisms are adaptive, while others are non-adaptive. For example, humor is considered an adaptive mechanism that enables an individual to bear difficult situations without harming him- or herself or others. Being able to laugh at yourself for your mistakes is certainly a lot healthier than worrying or feeling bad about them. One person we know has decided that it is his duty as a *gaijin* to amuse the Japanese at least once a day.

Sublimation is another constructive defense mechanism, in which the individual channels unwanted feelings into doing something constructive. Jogging every morning to cope with the feelings of anger or aggression experienced at work is an example of sublimation. Involvement in a service-oriented activity is also an adaptive mechanism. By helping others who are in need, you do not have the time to be overly preoccupied with your own problems. Non-adaptive defense mechanisms distract individuals from facing their own reactions and feelings, thus robbing them of the opportunity to change the distressing situation. The following are some of the typical defense mechanisms found among people living in a foreign culture.

Displacement Instead of expressing feelings directly, or addressing the cause of those feelings, individuals displace those emotions by taking their discomfort out on another person or object. For example, a businessperson feeling inadequate at work may express hostility toward his or her spouse, while a language teacher frustrated with the living conditions in Japan might take it out on the students. When you find that you are getting unreasonably upset at people, it's time to take a look at what may be upsetting you.

Projection When individuals experience feelings or reactions they believe are unacceptable, they tend to disown these feelings by "projecting" them onto another, believing it is the other person who has these feelings. For example, when some people feel irritated or frustrated but cannot accept these feelings, they tend to notice irritation in others. If you begin to feel that all Japanese are rude or insensitive, this might be a reflection of your own anger toward the daily stresses you experience.

Rationalization Finding justification for personal actions is one of the most common defense mechanisms. Telling yourself that it's okay to drink more because this is the way it is done in Japan is a typical example of rationalization. This mechanism prevents examination of the stresses that may be causing the problem behavior.

Denial In denial, the bothersome situation is pushed out of the individual's awareness. Denial, like other defense mechanisms, occurs on an unconscious level; therefore, the individual is unaware of the situations that might be creating stress. Many of us are taught that we should not complain about our situation. As a result, we have learned to accommodate to stressful situations while remaining unaware of the effects that situation may have on us. Denial has serious repercussions and can lead to burnout, sometimes pushing people to the point of total exhaustion.

Repression This is a process in which the individual disregards or withholds an idea or feeling from consciousness. While denial affects the perception of the immediate external reality, the repression mechanism interrupts the perception of the internal reality, i.e., what is going on inside. If you feel homesick but do not feel you have a right to feel this way, you can put homesickness out of your conscious mind (repress it) and deny that you have such feelings. However, these feelings remain in the subconscious mind and can eventually manifest themselves in physical symptoms or feelings of depression.

Although children appear to be less guarded about expressing their feelings, they too use certain defense mechanisms. Displacement is a common phenomenon seen among children and adolescents. Instead of expressing their sadness about leaving their home country, they tend to display aggressive behavior toward adults. The following are some defense mechanisms common to children.

Regression This defense mechanism occurs when children display behavior expected of children younger than they are. Sudden behavioral changes like thumb-sucking, bed-wetting, and whining are observed among children who are under stress but are unable to articulate or express their feelings.

Passive-Aggressive Behavior When children cannot express feelings such as anger in a direct way, those feelings will be expressed in an indirect way through their behavior. Uncooperative behaviors in the home, such as refusing to do what they are told to do or refusing to do their homework, are often signs that children have feelings that are unexpressed.

Acting Out Unlike regression and passive-aggressive behavior, in which feelings are indirectly expressed, this defense mechanism involves a direct expression of unconscious feelings. In acting out, children act impulsively to avoid being conscious of their feelings. Children who may be feeling depressed or anxious sometimes exhibit explosive behavior. This enables them to act out their feelings of discomfort instead of getting in touch with the actual anxiety or sadness they may be feeling inside. Acting out is a very common defense mechanism among adolescents.

Defense mechanisms are ways in which all of us unconsciously protect ourselves from both internal and external realities that create discomfort and pain. They are a natural part of life and a means of psychological survival, protecting us from feeling too vulnerable. While some defense mechanisms may be useful in the coping process, others are a hindrance. Once you become aware of the defense mechanisms you use, you will be able to accept the feelings behind those defenses and mobilize yourself to cope more constructively with the stresses affecting you.

For example, some people report feeling better just by calling a psychotherapist to make an appointment, then end up canceling it the next day. The mere acceptance of the need for help in coping with stress frees up the energy these individuals were consuming in denying the stress. This newly found energy can then be put to more creative use; as a result, they may finally decide that outside help is no longer necessary.

Sharing Your Experiences

Common to many foreigners here is the feeling of being alone and having to cope with the myriad difficulties of living and working in Japan. It is important to have others with whom you can share and talk about your experiences in order to release some of your feelings, to receive support and reassurance that you're not alone in what you are experiencing, and to gain an objective perspective on what is going on.

Close relationships in which you can share your feelings are sometimes difficult to establish, given the transitory nature of the foreign community. It takes time to establish close relationships, and sometimes people leave just as these relationships are being formed. When a close relationship has not yet been established, deciding how much to disclose about yourself can produce anxiety. It is possible to make close friends as long as you are willing to take the initiative. In fact, many people have found that it is often easier to establish friendships while living overseas because there is a sense that everyone is in the same boat. When facing the difficulties and challenges of living abroad, the only people who can really understand and empathize are those who have gone through what you are going through. It seems there are two choices: get to the level of intimacy or confidence with others early in the relationship, or never get there at all. You need to be conscious of this choice early on in the relationship process before the years slip quickly away and you discover your relationship was less than you might have wanted.

Groups are ideal in that they meet the majority of our needs for integration both within ourselves and within the community. They are especially beneficial for expats because of the tendency to retreat into our shells when we are trying to cope. Many participants in a group experience are surprised to discover how much they have in common with other members, even though they may come from different worlds in terms of nationality, age, religion, profession, education, or lifestyle.

In thinking about joining a group, remember that in addition to ready-made groups (see Chapter 6) it is also possible to start your own group that is geared to meet your specific needs. Begin simply by putting a notice of your intention in the local newspaper, newsletter, or bulletin board or on a website. The group can be formed with a response from as few as two or three committed individuals. Minimize overhead costs by meeting in your home. Frequent notices and word of mouth will increase membership, and the group will soon take on a life of its own. In fact, it will most likely continue to exist even after you have left Japan. Many thriving groups have had such humble beginnings; for example, Foreign Executive Women (FEW) began in this way.

For those who prefer one-to-one sharing, it is possible to actively seek a "buddy" to become a "share" partner. Such a relationship assures both parties of at least once-a-week face-to-face contact in which their lives are openly shared. Even if one person lives outside a major city, a weekly telephone conversation can serve much the same purpose. There is usually an agreement beforehand that the relationship must be a two-way street, and all sharing is to be kept strictly confidential. It should be noted that such partnerships need not be with someone in one's immediate social circle, because the sole purpose is to share feelings and experiences, rather than to socialize or to fit the usual definition of a "friendship," with its broader implications.

It should be kept in mind that not everyone "shares" in the same manner. For instance, there is a major difference between introverts and extroverts. Because introverts tend to prefer one-to-one, deep, intimate relationships, they may initially feel reluctant to share with people they feel they do not know well. Instead, they may prefer to take the necessary time and space to process their feelings internally before sharing them with others. On the other hand, extroverts are energized by others and prefer to share their feelings with many people. This more verbal, socially outward approach to dealing with problems often helps them to understand what and how they are feeling by the process of "thinking out loud."

The preference for introversion or extroversion can also have a cultural bias. Many non-Americans find extroverted Americans to be too loud, opinionated, and superficial, while the more introverted Japanese are often typecast by some Westerners as secretive, uncommunicative, or socially awkward.

Then there are those who prefer to deal with their feelings in an objective and analytical manner. Such people, especially if they are more introverted and cognitively oriented, may choose not to share their feelings with others, opting to deal with their problems by themselves and in their own way.

In general, when it comes to sharing our feelings with others, it is important to understand and accept our own style of relating. Only then can we become sensitive recipients of what others may or may not be willing to share with us.

Putting Things into Perspective

While living overseas, you can get so caught up in the process of adjusting that it is quite easy to lose sight of the overall picture and meaning of your life. Living as an expatriate, you might develop a distorted view of reality.

A large part of the expatriate community is a unique population, which finds itself in Japan as a result of personal motivations, accomplishments, and various privileges. None of the members of this group is on welfare. All are at least middle class or above, except for those who enter as foreign laborers. The majority are in good physical and mental health, well educated (college-educated or equivalent training), and well traveled. There are very few senior citizens and very few with physical or developmental disabilities.

The population certainly does not represent the average cross-section of society found in the home country. Living amidst a group of individuals with such exceptional abilities and characteristics affects its members in some significant ways.

Sometimes sensitivity toward the disadvantaged becomes dulled because of a lack of exposure to social problems. Expats sometimes become self-absorbed in the pursuit of their own personal goals. Later, along with feelings of emptiness, comes the realization that they've become indifferent to social concerns.

Like it or not, the expatriate community is an elite group. This is especially so in the corporate community, where most of the people fill executive positions. The pond may not be very big, but most of the fish are prizewinners. This is especially true in Japan, a nation considered one of the most desirable places for an overseas assignment because of its economic, political, educational, and cultural assets. Given the nature of this environment, it is very easy to lose a personal perspective of your strengths and to focus on what you don't have. You might feel overwhelmed by those who can speak better Japanese, live in larger homes, have higher executive positions, or have fascinating interests and backgrounds. If you're not careful, all this can turn into self-doubt, leading to the loss of a sense of self-worth.

You might also lose sight of the fact that life transitions do not come to a halt just because you're away from your home country. We all must deal with the personal changes that occur as the years pass by, wherever we are.

Children who arrive in Japan at the age of ten and remain for five years will have passed through the very important life stage of puberty by the time they return to their home country. Although it's more visible with children, adults also go through life-stage transitions while overseas. For those who come to Japan in their early to mid-twenties, like many English teachers, the next two to five years can be a crucial period for making decisions about career goals and relationship commitments. For others, the stay in Japan may coincide with midlife transition, a period in which many search for and redefine their life goals and values. For women this can be a period of dramatic physical and emotional changes. It is vitally important to focus on your own development and growth as these life stages present themselves.

When you have an overall perspective on your life, you can see how living overseas fits into the process. Then the stresses of living in another culture take on a new meaning. You might realize that you are not only coping with the stress brought about by living in Japan but also wrestling with issues that you would deal with no matter where you were living.

Finally, it is easy to lose sight of your values when you are caught up in the challenges of overseas living. You may become so absorbed in succeeding in your job or mastering the language and culture that you lose perspective on what is important in your life.

An Inventory of Personal Values is found on page 81. It is most helpful to sit down once in a while to take stock. Go through this inventory to learn if and how your values may have changed since your arrival in Japan and to decide if those changes are acceptable. You may find a need to alter your life situation in a way that is more consistent with your own personal values.

Constructive Activities

Exercise The benefits derived from exercise are immeasurable. It maintains and improves your physical health, helps relieve tension and depression, and brings into balance the physical and mental. Jogging, yoga, tennis, judo, qigong, aerobics, and swimming are but a few of the more popular forms of exercise that can be enjoyed in Japan.

With all these kinds of exercise available, walking is perhaps the best overall activity that can be easily accomplished on a daily basis. Walking can be done anywhere, anytime, and by anyone (young and old), with little or no training, and with or without companionship. And it's free of charge—no small matter in Japan. It can be done to suit your pace, avoiding competition and minimizing harmful mental and physical side effects. It is an activity that can be combined with walking the dog, shopping, talking to a friend, or listening to music or language tapes. Simply by investing thirty minutes to an hour each day, along with the price of a pair of walking shoes, you will reap the physical and mental benefits of walking. You'll learn that it can be a delightful way to get to know your environment, especially the side streets, where much of the charm of Japan is found.

Journal Keeping Writing in a journal is one activity that is extremely helpful in obtaining a perspective on life. Most of us have a tendency to distort or forget events—both good and bad—in addition to losing sight of the actual time span between the events themselves. By keeping a journal over an extended period of time, you can also identify cycles, both the physical (effects of the seasons, weather conditions, hormones, etc.) and the emotional (depression, anxiety, general ups and downs). Research has shown that writing about stress-provoking experiences increases the immune function as well.[3]

Recording your uncensored thoughts, feelings, actions, and reactions on a daily or weekly basis can be cathartic and serve as a means to identify, clarify, and reflect on (not judge) an event. This process enhances growth by enabling you to verify and accept personal elements that you might prefer to hide, especially from yourself. In recording dreams, we are also able to enter a dialogue with the unconscious—a storehouse of information, wisdom, and unexpected gifts.

To get started, you need only to buy a notebook, one that will stand the wear and tear of time and travel. Be sure to find a safe place to keep it. There are no rules; only remember to write in it on a regular basis and do not write for an audience. A journal is written by you and for you—it's your own bestseller.

Meditation and Relaxation Exercises Many books on meditation are available at English bookstores. During your next visit home, you might want to purchase audiotapes that guide you through the steps of relaxation exercises. Even though Eastern culture is known for its serenity, life in Japan, as you may already know, is extremely stressful. Reserving a few quiet moments for yourself at the end of each day can make a big difference in both the way you sleep and the way you feel when you wake up in the morning.

Skills Maintenance and Building Social Networks Life in Japan offers innumerable opportunities to develop new skills and interests. A major challenge some expatriates face is continued growth in the area of their previous training and interests. Though some opt to learn new skills and develop new interests, such as ikebana, shiatsu, photography, or teaching English, they also feel a need to maintain and build on the skills they brought with them from home.

Rather than limit your participation solely to membership in a particular group or organization, take an active role in the group's overall functioning. Many groups and organizations are in need of those who can make contributions. Leadership skills in the capacity of director, board member, consultant, or adviser are often in demand. Your professional expertise in such fields as law, nursing, accounting, linguistics, psychology, advertising, writing, editing, etc., may prove to be an invaluable asset. Upon returning home, your résumé not only will reflect a continuity of your professional life but will also have some unique and impressive additions.

In addition to making contributions to an existing group or organization, you can start your own, one that particularly focuses on an area of your personal or professional interests. Many expats have started reading groups, which are formed in the same manner as described earlier. Books chosen are usually the latest in one's field or ones that come highly recommended by a group member. Some groups choose a person to be responsible for leading the discussion and providing an overview of the book, while other groups are more loosely structured, without a designated leader. With such a diversified expat population, reading groups have proven to be both intellectually stimulating and culturally enriching.

Learning the Language Perhaps the greatest regret most expats have about living abroad is not having learned the language, believing that they were only going to be in Japan a few years. Countless stories abound in which expats have found themselves still in Japan five, ten, or twenty years longer than expected.

Learning Japanese is central to coping, in that it allows you to take a more active, rather than reactive, role in negotiating with everyday living and working in Japan. It will expand your horizons through friendships and increase your knowledge of the culture. Conversely, not knowing any Japanese is to be continually dependent on the mercy and goodwill of others for even the simplest things. Although this may sound like a dire prognosis, the good news is that learning Japanese is not as difficult as many would have you believe.

Just knowing the hiragana and katakana (the round and square forms of the Japanese syllabary) and a few hundred kanji can be sufficient to help you master your environment. To get your basic needs met, unless one works in Japanese, all it takes is conversational-level language ability. Many make the mistake of thinking they must know all the kanji or be able to speak in *keigo* (honorific language)—a feat that longtime expats (even those who are bilingual) find difficult to accomplish. As most Japanese are sympathetic to anyone trying to learn a second language (themselves included), you will be overwhelmed with positive feedback, however feeble your efforts.

Observing Rituals In an environment in which so many changes are taking place, it is important to have some sort of constancy in life. Rituals are behaviors that are repeated and predictable, with symbolic meaning beyond our rational comprehension. They may be personal, involving only ourselves, or they may be communal, involving family members or others.

Holiday rituals not only are fun for the children but are also important to all in marking the passage of time and for sheer celebration. Birthdays are not only about adding a year but also an initiation into new life stages. Bedtime stories for the kids, weekly family meetings, and monthly family outings reinforce family unity. For couples, having coffee together every morning, regardless of pressing demands, or going out to dinner once a week can strengthen the marital relationship. Spiritual rituals such as reading Scriptures, praying, meditating, and going to worship services connect us with the deepest parts of ourselves.

Whether or not we are aware of it, we all have our own set of rituals that give stability, continuity, direction, and meaning to life. It is important to set aside, on a regular basis, the time and space for carrying out such activities. This time is rightfully yours; you are the only one who has the power to secure it. Guard it with your life.

Emotional Inventory[4]

- accepted
- accepting
- affectionate
- afraid
- alarmed
- alienated from others
- alienated from self
- angry
- anxious

anxious to please others
apathetic
appreciated
attractive
awkward
comfortable
competent
confident
confused
creative
curious
defeated
dependent
depressed
deprived
disappointed in myself
disappointed with others
dominated
eager to impress others
easygoing
embarrassed
envious
excited
exhilarated
failure, like a
fearful
feminine
flirtatious
frustrated
grateful
gratified by personal
  accomplishment
guilty
hateful
hopeful
hopeless
hostile

humorous
hurt
hypochondriacal
  (overly anxious about health)
immobilized
impatient
inadequate
incompetent
inconsistent
in control
indecisive
independent
inferior
inhibited
insecure
involved
jealous
judgmental
lonely
manipulated
masculine
misunderstood
needy
optimistic
out of control
overcontrolled
peaceful
phony
possessive
preoccupied
prejudiced
pressured
rejected
religious
remorseful
restrained
rewarded

sad
secure
self-pity, deserving of
shy
sincere
sluggish
sorry for self
stubborn
stupid
suicidal
supported
supportive
sympathetic
tender
terrified
threatened

tolerant
torn
two-faced
ugly
unappreciated
understanding
ungifted
unresponsive
uptight
used by others
useless
victimized
violent
weary of living
weepy
wishy-washy

Other Emotions:

_____
_____
_____

Inventory of Personal Values[5]

Mark with O those values that correspond to your own, and X those you least accept. Rank your five most strongly held values.

Getting ahead
Being honest
Succeeding in a job
Working hard
Enjoying my family
Taking care of my parents
Being free
Pursuing my happiness
Accumulating goods and wealth
Educating myself

Developing my spiritual side
Developing my emotional side
Enjoying leisure time
Helping humankind and working for the betterment of society
Winning
Honoring my word, oath, promises, etc.
Saving time
Being productive
Developing new relationships
Being tolerant
Being loyal to my country

Others Values:

_____
_____
_____

Have your values changed since your arrival?
If there have been changes, are you comfortable with them?
If they are not acceptable, what changes do you plan to make?
What values are most important for those in my family?
What values are most important for my friends, colleagues, and partner, who may be of another nationality?

6 Reaching Out

A tree that it takes both arms to encircle grew from a tiny rootlet. A many-storied pagoda is built by placing one brick upon another brick. A journey of three thousand miles is begun by a single step.
—Lao-Tzu
Chinese philosopher

A person's coping mechanism, which may mean the difference between merely surviving or thriving in a foreign country, is often determined by the ability to reach out to others for support, guidance, and, in some cases, professional help. While some people are better than others at networking or knowing how to use the system, most of us would prefer to use such skills for the purpose of helping others rather than ourselves.

Why Not?

The simple truth is that when it comes to accepting help, it is easier to give than to receive. Reaching out in order to get help for ourselves can sometimes be an uncomfortable, anxiety-provoking, even embarrassing experience, making us feel vulnerable, helpless, or foolish. For Westerners (especially men), who are raised to be self-sufficient and self-reliant, independent, and physically and emotionally strong, it is hard to admit that one needs help, let alone seek outside assistance.

Similarly, many Japanese people may find it equally difficult to receive help and often go to any extent to avoid being an imposition *(gomeiwaku)* on others. One reason for this attitude is the fear that they may be indebted to the giver for the rest of their lives. In Japanese culture, the person who offers help is also expected to be responsible for the welfare of those they help, especially if they saved someone's life, so it is understandable why many well-meaning Japanese are reluctant to be on the receiving or giving end of such a relationship. Whether it is the Western teaching of "keeping a stiff upper lip" or the Japanese notion of *gaman* (perseverance at all costs), the act of reaching out to others for help does not come naturally to most of us.

While the perception of reaching out is often a negative one—characterized as a loss of face, self-esteem, and control—the reality is that we often gain an expansion of our personalities and worldview by doing so. The result is usually a healthier sense of who we are, not who we think we are or wish to be. As expats and as members of the human race, we learn that we are all in this predicament together—not a small realization, considering that deep down most of us believe that everyone else is coping better with living in Japan and with life in general.

The first step in reaching out to others is the most difficult, as we must come to terms with all the assumptions we have about ourselves. As expats we need to ask, "What is our perceived image or role vis-à-vis living and working in Japan? Were we sent here as disseminators of services, products, expertise, knowledge, goodwill, or a way of life? Or did we come as rugged individualists, adventurers, or trailblazers?" The degree and intensity with which we identify with our persona—the mask or face that we put on for the outside world—will often determine how readily and in what manner we are willing to accept help.

The Need to Be Connected

Though the saying "No man is an island" may sound trite, many find that they are living isolated lives, particularly in Japan. To help prevent such a situation, it is important to have a variety of relationships. The following are five different types of relationships that are important for our sense of well-being and growth:

> Relationships that offer daily contact, such as those with shopkeepers, the person at the checkout counter, apartment managers, etc., validate that you are a member of the local community.
>
> Relationships with neighbors, or those with whom you can engage in small talk about the weather or current events, foster sociability.

Deeper-level relationships expand your horizons and provide stimulation. These include contact with coworkers or people belonging to the same group with whom you can talk about life events and share information (weekend activities, diets, trips, shopping, etc.).

Relationships with close friends are those in which you can share your problems, disappointments, hopes, and joys. They help develop your capacity to trust others.

Your intimate friends and family members are a special group of people with whom you share the deepest parts of yourself, including your weaknesses and fears. They remind us of our fragility and of our need for one another.[1]

All five types of interactions have something different to offer, and it is ideal to have relationships on all levels. Surprisingly, a fair number of expats find themselves having relationships on only one or two levels. Introverts often maintain the attitude that the kind of "small talk" found on levels one and two is superficial and a waste of time. They prefer intimacy at levels three, four, and five. On the other hand, extroverts are stimulated by having many friends and acquaintances and have a tendency to spread their time and energy very thinly. They may be unable to sustain the degree of intimacy required for the types of relationships at levels four and five.

Living overseas, it is sometimes difficult to have relationships with shopkeepers and neighbors because of the language barrier. Daily contact with these people, however, is important because it provides a sense of belonging and an opportunity to share warm and friendly feelings. You may want to make a point of dining out once a week at a local sushi restaurant or shopping at a mom-and-pop shop, instead of at convenience or department stores, so as to become known on a first-name basis. Even a friendly exchange with a total stranger can be a nurturing experience. One American woman stated:

> It just made my day yesterday. I was tired and I got in the taxi, and the driver was friendly and commented on how well I spoke Japanese. That was just the thing I needed.

Community Resources

One way to obtain all five types of relating is to take advantage of what the community has to offer. It is reassuring to know that although the total number of expats in Japan is comparatively small, the variety and quality of assistance—albeit changeable—is considerable.

The following sections help identify the kind of support available to the foreign community and its relevance for our mental and physical health. All institutions, programs, and services that have been chosen here have stood the test of time. In cases where phone numbers may have changed, or for a more complete listing, up-to-date information can be found in the English-language newspapers; the TELL (Tokyo English Life Line) calendar; local journals and magazines; directories; books found in the English-language section of bookstores; through telephone services, clubs, or associations; or at embassies and churches. The proliferation of websites on the Internet has also created many excellent sources for information.

Orientation Programs and Services

There is no doubt that for the newcomer who is planning to live and work in Japan, participation in an orientation program is worth the time and effort. These programs not only help you through the various stages of culture shock but can also provide useful information, ranging from how to use the transportation system to relevant historical and cultural facts about Japan. Think of orientation programs or services as preventive medicine. They are a positive step in the direction of self-help, enabling you to feel more in control, and aid in gaining a sense of mastery over your new environment and the expatriate living situation. For some, these programs can be a decisive factor in getting off to a good start—a significant achievement, considering that the newcomer is faced with half a dozen unfamiliar situations at once.

If your sponsor, whether it is a business, church, embassy, or academic institution, does not provide an in-house orientation program, other options are available. Within the foreign community, there are institutions, organizations, and businesses that offer orientation programs and services for individuals and their families.

For the very newly arrived, there is Welcome Furoshiki, a service sponsored by various companies. A representative will visit your hotel or home, free of charge, and you will receive a bundle of information, including questions and answers about living in Tokyo, Yokohama, Osaka, and Kobe. To arrange a private visit, call:

Tokyo and Yokohama	(03) 5472-7074
Osaka, Kobe, and Kyoto	(06) 6441-2584

In addition to receiving a home visit, one should consider calling or visiting any one of the major churches, synagogues, or mosques. They are often helpful in orienting a newcomer to the expatriate community. Most have informal coffee hours, lectures, information about community resources, and reading materials about Japan. They are open to the public and are excellent places to meet potential friends, who may be another newcomer, an old-timer, or a Japanese returnee. In general, even if one is not of any particular religious persuasion, places of worship, along with embassies, are the pillars of any expat community, with their histories, continuity, and convenient locations. While embassies offer help based on one's nationality, religious institutions represent a cross-section of the expat community, providing programs and assistance to anyone regardless of nationality, age, or social and economic status. The following are but a few of such religious institutions:

Franciscan Chapel Center	(03) 3401-2141
Islamic Center Japan	(03) 3460-6169
Jewish Community of Japan	(03) 3400-2559
Saint Alban's Anglican/Episcopal Church	(03) 3431-8534
St. Paul's International Lutheran Church	(03) 3261-3740
Tokyo Baptist Church	(03) 3461-8425
Tokyo Union Church	(03) 3400-0047
Yokohama Union Church	(045) 651-5177
Kobe Union Church	(078) 871-6844

The Women's Group of the Tokyo American Club sponsors a popular orientation program twice a year known as Tokyo Here and Now, which is open to the public. For information about the cost and the exact dates, call (03) 3224-3691.

The Yokohama International Women's Club hosts a one-day newcomers' orientation program each September for those living in the Yokohama area. The number to call is (045) 753-7485.

Those living in the Kansai area can find a program known as Bloom Where You Are Planted, sponsored by the Community House and Information Centre (CHIC) in Kobe. For more information, call (078) 857-6540.

For more comprehensive orientation programs, there are several businesses that specialize in various aspects of living overseas. There are also individuals who, having successfully gone through the orientation process, are now offering their assistance. These services may include "look-see" trips prior to one's move, practical help with the relocation process, and follow-up care. As these programs are subject to change, check the newspapers and expat-oriented journals that advertise these services.

Tokyo English Life Line (TELL)

In a category all its own, this nonprofit, church-sponsored organization is affiliated with Life Line International and is fully accredited by the Samaritan Institute in the United States. Since its inception in 1973, TELL has provided three distinct services for the expatriate community.

First, perhaps the best-known service is telephone counseling. The most frequently discussed problem areas are marital difficulties, depression, male-female relationships, legal and visa advice, employment problems, education and career problems, health issues, and loneliness. A Filipino Line is also available to provide counseling in Tagalog and other Filipino dialects at (03) 3968-4071. A call to TELL can often ease feelings of alienation as well as help sort through one's problems, including identifying the problem. Through the helping process, there is no attempt to impose a particular philosophy. All information given is held in strictest confidence, and the caller may remain anonymous. For more information about the times of operation, call (03) 3968-4099. Should this number change for any reason, consult any of the English-language newspapers.

Second, TELL offers referral services, including the names of medical doctors, therapists, dentists, orientation programs, etc. When asking for a referral, make sure you receive the name and number of more than one service from which to choose. Information about support groups, crisis centers, hot lines, and women's shelters are also available and are continually updated and expanded for the ever-changing community. TELL also has telephone numbers for Japanese-sponsored programs, such as the Foreign Residents Advisory Center, which offers assistance in five languages. TELL's ability to make referrals may include areas other than Tokyo, Yokohama, Kyoto, Osaka, and Kobe.

In order to maintain a high level of professionalism, TELL provides another service: training its volunteer counselors in a sixty-hour course, one commencing in February and the other in September. The volunteers must also complete a twenty-four-hour apprenticeship as part of their training. Being a TELL volunteer can be an enriching experience, enabling you to learn more about yourself and the community in which you live and providing an opportunity to return the help you may have received in the course of your stay here.

TELL also provides community education in the form of workshops, lectures, and a quarterly community mental-health newsletter. As you can see from the variety of services this organization offers, if you're looking for help, it's best to remember: When in doubt, call TELL. They may not always be able to answer all your questions, but you can be assured that they will take the care, time, and energy to try to be of service to you.

Support Groups

The importance of having an ongoing support network while living overseas cannot be overemphasized. It is the major item you left behind in your home country, and it cannot be totally replaced. It is absolutely essential that you put together a support community of your own, especially if you are not a part of a closely knit, highly structured institution or organization such as the embassy, the military, or the missionary community. Experience has shown that those who are not a part of such a support system are more at risk if and when a problem arises.[2] As with orientation programs, belonging to some sort of group during your stay in Japan should be considered preventive medicine.

In addition to the obvious social, educational, therapeutic, or spiritual advantages of belonging to a group, there are many other benefits. A group provides structure, routine, and a sense of continuity in that you can count on being with a group of people at a specific place and time for a certain number of times per week or month. These are especially important factors for newcomers who feel uprooted. On a deeper level, you are accountable to the group for missing a session or for dropping out. Similarly, the group is accountable to you. Regardless of the type of group, the resulting two-way interaction leads to a sense of belonging and to shared fellowship. As one Canadian newcomer noted:

> I was so miserable when I arrived here that I couldn't even get out of bed, let alone the house. However, things began to change when a friend asked me to join a group. At first it was hard, since I really didn't want to see or be with anyone. Then all of a sudden I began to feel better about myself and about being in Japan. I guess you could say that just showing up somewhere did the trick for me.

Sources of support are available in your community; at places of employment, schools, religious institutions, and clubs (both social and athletic); and in other associations, e.g., professional, business, alumni, and public service. The following section illustrates the kinds of groups that are available within the expat community. These groups are open to the public and are either free or levy a minimal charge to cover expenses. Keep in mind that some numbers may be an individual's home phone number and are likely to change over time. TELL will, in most instances, have the current number if changes have been made.

One type of group is for educational purposes, whether to learn about Japan or a new skill or craft. By attending classes, one also receives support through shared activities and the ensuing friendships.

Tokyo Union Church (sponsored by the TUC Women's Society) has a popular and extensive program of more than fifty courses, including shiatsu, bridge, *washi* craft, ikebana, cooking, exercise, and Japanese pottery, as well as special classes covering various aspects of living in Japan. Nursery care is also available. For more information, call (03) 3400-0942.

For those living in the Kansai area, the Osaka YWCA has what is known as a Cross-Cultural Project. It offers courses in various Japanese crafts and the chance to participate in cultural events like the *hina* doll lunch or in one-day or overnight trips to historical spots. For more information, call (06) 6872-0505.

In Kobe, the Community House and Information Centre (CHIC) offers classes in Japanese language and culture, Western and Japanese arts and crafts, cooking, and health-related courses like shiatsu and qigong. There are also classes for children. Call (078) 857-6540 for information about its complete program.

Another type of group you'll find in Japan focuses on putting your particular talents and interests to use by providing entertainment for others. There is always a need for performers in the foreign community as well as for people who can be involved in the practical aspects of putting together a performance.

Sweet Adelines	(03) 3390-4945
Tokyo International Players (TIP)	(03) 3447-1981
Tokyo International Singers	(044) 833-9258
Tokyo Theater for Children	(03) 3402-3645

Professional-interest groups enable members to keep abreast of trends and events in their field of interest. They also offer support and training and provide an opportunity to address the issues and concerns of working in Japan. For more information, call (or fax, where indicated) the following numbers:

Foreign Executive Women (FEW)	090-7216-5171
	www.few.gol.com
Foreign Lawyers Association of Japan	3527-0988
Japan Association of Language Teachers (JALT):	*See announcement section of The Japan Times*
Kaisha Society	(03) 5562-0382
Society of Writers, Editors, and Translators (SWET)	(045) 314-9324

Some support groups are centered on personal issues. They offer direct emotional support for their members and can be an invaluable source of healing. To make further inquiries, call:

Akebono Kai (breast cancer support group)	(03) 3792-1204
Alcoholics Anonymous	(03) 3971-1471
Overeaters Anonymous	(03) 5605-9425
Prenatal and Infant Death Support Group	(03) 3499-3111
Support in Grief	(03) 3401-2141

The largest category of support groups is composed of those centered on special status interests and concerns. In addition to the groups listed below, there are many others that operate throughout Japan. Call TELL for further information.

Amnesty International	(03) 3203-1050
Association of Foreign Wives of Japanese	(045) 753-7485 (nationwide)
Friends of the Earth	(03) 3951-1081
La Leche International	(03) 3410-6554
Marriage Encounter	(03) 3401-2141

The final list includes the service-oriented groups. Reaching out to others by volunteering your special skills, talents, funds, or time can be a personally enriching experience. If you are interested, call the following:

College Women's Association of Japan	(03) 3444-2167
International Social Services of Japan	(03) 3760-3471
Japan Help Line	0120-461-997
Japan International Volunteer Center	(03) 3834-2388
Refugees International Japan	(03) 5500-3093
Welcome Furoshiki Representative	(03) 5472-7074 (Tokyo); (06) 6441-2584 (Osaka)
Yokohama International Women's Club	(045) 753-7485

Medical and Psychiatric Help

Sometimes we need to seek professional medical or psychiatric assistance to help cope with problems that either are or seem overwhelming. This may be for ourselves or for a friend we are concerned about.

It is not uncommon to find that those who seek psychotherapeutic help also have very real medical problems. This is not surprising given the fact that Western researchers have produced significant evidence to suggest that there is a mind-body interaction (an old Asian concept) and that many problems are an interplay of physical and psychological forces. We know that when we are not in the best physical health (because of a poor diet or a lack of exercise or proper sleep), we may experience a change in mood or our sense of well-being. As a starting point, to help rule out the possibility that one's distress is only psychological, it never hurts to first undergo a thorough medical checkup.

Specifically, there are a number of medical conditions that should be checked out if you are suffering from intermittent or chronic symptoms related to depression, anxiety, or mental disorientation in addition to having mild or uncomfortable physical ailments. The most common are allergies (pollen, food, chemical, and environmental), PMS (premenstrual syndrome), hypoglycemia, chronic fatigue syndrome, hypothyroidism, candidiasis, and seasonal affective disorder (SAD). Unless a physician is a specialist in treating these conditions, sufferers are often improperly diagnosed and sent from one doctor to another, only to be told it's all in their head. As a result, many end up seeing a psychiatrist (and usually given medication) or receiving long-term therapy with little relief. Such medical conditions are often triggered or exacerbated by the stress of living overseas in addition to being in a new environment.

Medical facilities in Japan not only give general physical examinations but will make appropriate referrals for diagnostic tests (X rays, blood tests, stress tests, etc.). If you wish to be tested for thyroid function or allergies, it is up to you to request it, because many tests, such as Pap smears and mammograms, are not routinely conducted in Japan.

Likewise, when the results are back, it may once again be left up to you to decide what form of treatment would be best for you. In doing so, make sure you obtain at least a second opinion, and possibly a third, in your home country. In attempting to make the best possible choice, many expats have used the Internet to gather information about the symptoms, treatment, and prognosis of an illness, as well as the latest research in the field.

Another avenue to explore is an alternative approach to healing. This is especially helpful in treating chronic conditions, such as those previously mentioned, in which medication often has not been helpful and in some cases even harmful, particularly with regard to possible side effects. Many debilitating ailments have responded well to nutritional supplements, a change in diet and exercise, and Oriental treatments such as acupuncture, shiatsu, and qigong. In fact, expats have been known to return to their home countries considerably healthier than when they left, having taken advantage of what the East has to offer. Numerous studies have concluded that Japanese women generally do not suffer the effects of menopause or breast cancer to the degree that Western women are afflicted, primarily because of the traditional Japanese diet. A good reference book on alternative approaches to healing is *Healthy Healing* by Linda Rector-Page (Healthy Healing Publications, 1997), which lists more than two hundred medical conditions, along with drugless approaches to curing or managing one's mental and physical conditions.

In the event that your distress is not entirely physical, most clinics and larger hospitals can provide, upon request, medication in the form of tranquilizers or antidepressants to help you get through a difficult time. This may mean consulting a psychiatrist for medication while seeing a psychotherapist to talk about your problems. You should not feel uncomfortable with such an arrangement, because only medical doctors can prescribe medication, and most Japanese psychiatrists working in medical facilities do not have the time or language ability to conduct ongoing psychotherapy.

The following hospitals and clinics offer medical and psychiatric assistance. When calling for information, be sure to check on what type of insurance they will take.

Juntendo University Hospital	(03) 3813-3111
Kanto-Chuo Hospital	(03) 3429-1171
Keio University Hospital	(03) 3353-1211
Seibo Byoin (International Catholic Hospital)	(03) 3951-1111
St. Luke's International Hospital	(03) 3541-5151
Japan Baptist Hospital (Kyoto)	(075) 781-5191
Yodogawa Christian Hospital (Osaka)	(06) 6322-2250

In addition to those listed above, call TELL to obtain further information regarding medical facilities and the names of specialists in any given field. The AMDA International Medical Information Center also provides referrals to doctors and hospitals and information about the Japanese medical system. For those in Tokyo, call (03) 5285-8088; Kansai residents can call (06) 6636-2333. In addition, an excellent reference book titled *Japan Health Handbook* by Meredith Maruyama, Louise Shimizu, and Nancy Tsurumaki (Kodansha International, 1999) provides a wealth of information on the various aspects of obtaining medical and psychiatric help in Japan.

Generally, when looking for help, remember not to choose a health-care professional based on geographic proximity or language ability alone. There are many fine physicians in Japan—some who are preeminent in their area of expertise. If language is a problem, do not hesitate to ask a bilingual friend to accompany you.

Counseling and Psychotherapy

Professional psychological help is sought for both long-standing problems and short-term adjustment problems. Problem areas addressed in counseling or psychotherapy include marital difficulties; a bothersome personal symptom or self-defeating behavior; a life-stage-related difficulty (adolescence, midlife, or retirement); a crisis situation such as a divorce, abortion, serious illness, relocation, or death; or a vague, undefinable feeling of unrest or dissatisfaction with one's life. Many consult a therapist as a "reality check" in order to be reassured that they are still "normal," having gone through so many changes as a result of coming to Japan. Any musings or threats of suicide require prompt attention.

To help deal with these and other problems, psychiatrists, psychiatric or clinical social workers, psychologists (clinical and educational), and pastoral counselors are the mental-health professionals most commonly consulted by members of the foreign community. Keep in mind that these professional titles do not necessarily reflect the only type of services offered by a particular therapist. For example, a psychologist who possesses a variety of individual therapy skills may also be a group therapist, a clinical social worker may be a career counselor, a psychiatrist may be a hypnotherapist, and a pastoral counselor may also be a licensed marriage counselor.

Often the most reliable method of finding an appropriate therapist is to ask your friends for a referral, especially those who have been here long enough to know which therapists are highly recommended. Other factors that may be important in selecting a therapist include the following: second-language ability, nationality, religious orientation, age, sex, and the number of years spent practicing in Japan. The latter includes not only whether the therapist has gone through the necessary readjustment process but how long he or she plans to be in Japan—an important consideration for long-term residents. Generally, after considering insurance, the location of the therapist's office, and the schedules of both parties, it is often not a complicated process to narrow the choice to a single therapist.

The following counseling services offer professional and confidential therapeutic help in the broad categories of individual, marital, and family therapy. Some of these services will also provide the names and telephone numbers of other qualified therapists in the community whose expertise, office location, and availability may be more appropriate for a particular client. When calling, leave your name and phone number on the answering machine (please speak slowly and clearly) so that your call can be returned as soon as possible.

AMI Counseling	(03) 3448-1272
Counseling International	(03) 3408-5476

International Social Services	(03) 3760-3471
TELL Community Counseling Service	(03) 3498-0231

In the Kansai area, you will find the following counseling services:

Aoibashi Family Clinic (Kyoto)	(075) 431-9150
Dawn Center	
(Osaka Women's Prefectural Center)	(06) 6910-8588
International Counseling Centre	(078) 856-2201

In addition to the specialized mental-health services available to the English-speaking expatriate community, psychological help is also available through the guidance counselors and educational specialists at the international schools, from pastoral counselors in the international churches, and from therapists in private practice. Many of these helping professionals have been known to the foreign community for a considerable length of time and are very much a part of the community mental-health system.

7 Departure

For me, going,
For you, staying,
Two autumns.
    —Buson
    Japanese poet

The tickets have been purchased, side trips en route planned, packers notified, "for sale" ads placed in local newspapers, and the general dismantling process has begun. The time has come to make preparations for the return trip home. The energy and thought once used to create a home here in Japan must now be redirected to tearing things down, to beginning the process over again.

No matter how many times you have moved, even if only across the street or on to bigger and better things, there is nothing more unsettling than seeing your cherished belongings taken out of familiar settings and put away in cardboard boxes. For many, just the act of packing can be depressing, bringing to mind other times of closure and transition in life. But it is also a time for new beginnings, making decisions about what items to keep and what to give away, sell, or throw out.

Reverse Culture Shock: An Overview

As difficult as the process of relocation may be, there is a growing body of evidence that strongly suggests that one is also likely to encounter difficulties upon returning home. This experience is known as reverse culture shock, and it can be even more challenging than the process of culture shock.

The concept of reverse culture shock was first formulated in 1974 by Richard Brislin and H. Van Buren of the East-West Center, Hawaii.[1] Since then, literally hundreds of studies have been conducted to expand the existing knowledge of the phenomenon and to develop training programs designed to ease the impact of the reentry process.[2]

Reverse culture shock may be felt in a number of different ways. For expatriates who have just returned to their home country, some of the more common characteristics are feelings of boredom, apathy, problems starting a new project or job, problems picking up from where one had left off, and general feelings of anxiety and depression.

For some people, there may be a painful realization that they really are unable to go home again. Some who find themselves in this situation decide to return to the country they had just left behind or to move to a third culture, thus becoming more or less permanent expatriates. Although this may sound like an overly dramatic response to living overseas, the challenges of reverse culture shock are real. But with some understanding of the processes involved in returning home, the returnee is better able to anticipate and thereby cope with the many challenges that so unexpectedly present themselves.

There are several factors that are unique to reverse culture shock, as opposed to culture shock. First and foremost, most individuals expect things to be different when they go to an unfamiliar culture, but they do not expect any differences when they return to their home countries. This fact alone catches them off guard and upsets the reentry process.

A second and perhaps more obvious factor is that after living in a foreign culture, expatriates themselves have undergone some changes as a result of the experience. These changes, whether large or small, are mostly hidden from them, and they may feel, aside from having survived some stressful situations, that they are the same easygoing or uptight people that they were before going overseas.

There is no doubt that in the process of making cultural adjustments, expatriates are forced to go beyond personal limits and thereby develop new aspects of their personality. The easygoing person may have become more cautious, while the uptight person may have learned to take more things in stride. While this type of personality change may prove beneficial to the expatriate while abroad, the enlargement or enhancement could cause a strain on relationships back home. Friends, relatives, and colleagues may prefer to see the returnee unchanged in any respect.

Not only has the expatriate changed, but home has also changed. Significant shifts in economic, social, religious, and political systems now occur within the span of a few years, as do rapid changes in individual and group values. These combine to require the returnee to reevaluate many personal belief systems. Furthermore, family dynamics within the extended family may have changed during a person's absence, and the returnee must establish new roles and ways of relating to relatives.

The final factor unique to reverse culture shock is the feeling of hurt and disappointment returnees may feel in reaction to the general lack of interest regarding their overseas experience on the part of friends, relatives, and colleagues.[3] Returnees might find that no one shows interest in their fascinating experiences in Bali or Bangkok, let alone empathizing or understanding their "homesickness" for Japan. Returnees must take it upon themselves to show interest in domestic affairs. After all, the others reason, it is the travelers who have missed much during their absence.

The W-Curve of Cultural Adjustment

The W-curve of cultural adjustment is an extension of the U-curve hypothesis, taking into account the process of reentry.[4] Although it has been documented that most expatriates go through an experience similar to the seven phases of the W-curve, there will always be those who do not fit into this particular model. Most expatriates, however, will experience the phases associated with reverse culture shock, with modifications in the length of time between each phase and in the intensity of the highs and lows.

Figure 3 and the subsequent narrative are offered to illustrate, in a highly stylized manner, the hypothesis based upon the expatriate situation in Japan. It is used only to help the returnee conceptualize an often troubling experience.

As noted in Chapter 2, the third phase of cultural adjustment is a period when the expatriate reaches a relatively high level of satisfaction. For many, this can be close to, the same as, or surpass the level of well-being experienced prior to coming to Japan. Having gone through the honeymoon phase (1) and the disappointment phase (2), and having arrived at the cultural integration/adjustment phase (3), which is characteristic of the overall cultural adjustment process, the expatriate who begins to think about and plan for the return home enters the fourth phase known as the "second honeymoon."

The W-Curve of Cultural Adjustment

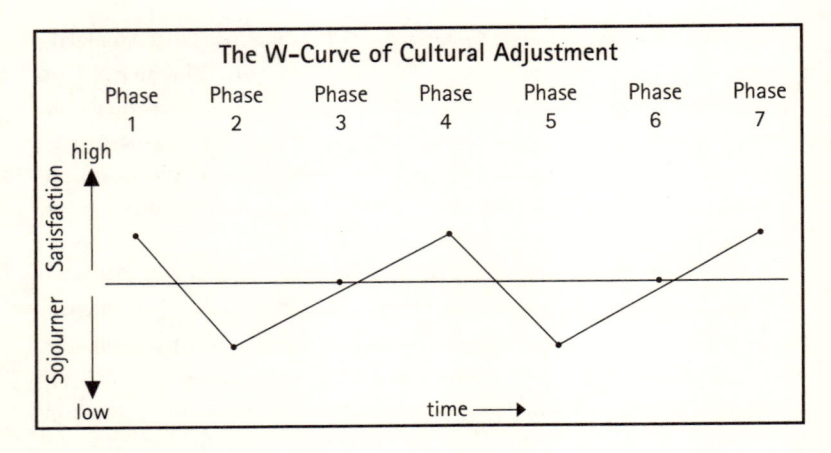

Figure 3

Depending on the level of sojourn satisfaction in Phase 3, there are generally three reactions to the prospect of leaving Japan. The first reaction is a feeling that despite all the ups and downs, it will be good to get back home to family, friends, and country. The second is a practical, matter-of-fact approach wherein the returnee feels that although living in Japan has been a very worthwhile experience, it is nevertheless time to head home, especially for the sake of the children. In the third response, the expatriate does not want to return home, realizing that the expatriate lifestyle is more satisfying than the one left behind.

Despite the variety of reactions to leaving Japan, the reality is that once again the sojourners find themselves going through a honeymoon phase similar to the one they experienced upon coming to Japan. For some, there may be a feeling of well-being, which accompanies the knowledge that the end is in sight—that an assignment, contract, or mission has been successfully accomplished. For others, it is the expectation of starting a new chapter of their lives. Things that may have been irritating about Japan are now seen with more objectivity, empathy, or affection.

In the final months, efforts are often made to see the "real" Japan, stay at the oldest *ryokan* (traditional inn), buy another *tansu* (chest), or try eating *fugu* (blowfish). The frenzied sightseeing (both in and out of Japan) is interspersed with many *sayonara* parties, reminding expatriates that perhaps, in the end, the Japanese did appreciate their years of service here, quite possibly more so than did those back home. Mixed with all these activities are the fantasies: the house with a yard, the upcoming trip to Europe, and the friends and relatives who eagerly await the expatriate's return. Even those who do not want to return (especially children) will find it difficult not to get caught up in the commotion of the "second honeymoon" phase. As one American woman in her thirties who has lived in Japan for three years stated:

> You know you and the children don't want to leave, but somehow you have to get psyched up to get through it. The bottom line is to picture all your furniture gone. Then you can't do anything else but imagine what lies ahead, and sooner or later you find yourself thinking about the good aspects of going home.

Once back home, the afterglow of the Japan experience may linger. Returning to familiar haunts, reestablishing old acquaintances, waiting for the household-goods shipment to arrive, and thinking about redoing the home with an Oriental touch all add to the general excitement of the first few months. As many returnees do not return to the exact job situation they left behind, there can also be an air of anticipation about what the changes will bring—perhaps a promotion or a transfer to another city and a new home. This is a time filled with hopes, plans, and activities but also, sometimes, with waiting. After a six-year sojourn in Japan, one American wife in her fifties wrote:

> I'm sitting here in this motel just waiting for something to happen. My husband is at corporate headquarters checking out the job situation. Since our arrival we've been in limbo land, a month already. All our things except clothing are in storage in Japan, and I feel suspended.

Somewhere between three and six months, the novelty of being back home begins to wear off. Some experience this much sooner. One psychologist in her forties, who returned to the United States after two years in Japan, wrote:

> When I first returned, I felt only vaguely here. I felt as though my spirit was floating over the Pacific—not really home yet—for a long time. The feeling was strong for six months; it has not totally left me one year later. I feel deeply attached (spiritually) to Japan, to the land, to the gardens of Ryoanji . . .

Some find it a shock to realize that being home is business as usual. In fact, no longer being thought of as a *gaijin,* with all its ascribed meaning of specialness, can feel like a real demotion in social status, not to mention the very real loss of the "perks" to which one had become accustomed in Japan. The perks may not have been material objects or conditions but an opportunity to live in an environment where one is exposed to different values and ways of thinking. A family who had returned home to Europe after a four-year stay reported that they were initially surprised to find that their fellow countrymen seemed so narrow-minded and rigid. They hadn't realized, until they returned home, how open-minded they had become while living in Japan.

For others, the home country may seem to be more run-down than they remembered. The noticeable potholes in the road, along with the unkempt cars that would never pass a *shaken* (inspection) check in Japan, become a sore sight to the returnee's eyes. The lack of service and politeness toward the customer leave some feeling continually outraged. Returnees often find themselves standing in front of a taxi, forever waiting for the door to open automatically, as it did in Japan.

Perhaps most disturbing is when well-intentioned friends and relatives start to ask the returnee about the sojourn in Japan, only to interrupt the response with their own news about Uncle Charlie's broken leg. It can be a shock for returnees to realize that they are expected to pick up the same conversation begun years ago.

The process of readjusting to an old, known environment may prove to be more challenging than that of adjusting to a new and unknown situation. As with learning about a new culture, the returnee may have to relearn some of the home culture's rules and expectations. Returnees to the United States often find they must relearn assertiveness and forcefulness in order to be noticed and heard, a demeanor they had learned to tone down while living in Japan. In the second phase of cultural adjustment, the newly arrived expatriate wanted the Japanese to accommodate, to be more like "us." In this stage of reverse culture shock, the returnee may be asking, Why can't our train system be more like Japan's? Statements to the boss or to colleagues such as "Well, in Japan we did it this way" can unintentionally slip out and are not usually well received.

But if returnees can weather Phase 5 of reverse culture shock, then Phase 6 can be a creative time, during which all that has been learned from the overseas experience can be integrated into their overall lifestyle. The returned expat has gained a more balanced and enriched view of things.

In Phase 7 the returnee can reap permanent benefits from the sojourn abroad and achieve an even higher level of satisfaction than that experienced prior to the move to Japan. Even those who do not want to leave Japan will, after one or two years (much sooner for children), make peace with being back in their home country. A psychologist wrote:

> What was good about coming home? For my husband, driving a car and watching football and basketball. For my teenage son, being like the others instead of experiencing himself as different and as a representative of America. For me, I guess I feel that I have a little more leeway here somehow . . . to just say what I feel, be myself—mucking up is not so bad. I don't have to devote so much energy to other people's feelings—to looking after them or accommodating them. For me the best thing about being home is that I am now close to my extended family.

Coping with Reverse Culture Shock

One exercise that is highly effective in helping to cope with reverse culture shock is the "work of worrying." The concept behind the exercise is that if you were to put in sufficient time worrying about an upcoming event, such as returning to your home country, then the gap between your expectation and reality would be narrowed, thus minimizing the effects of reverse culture shock.[5]

In carrying out the work of worrying, it is useful to think about the following broad areas and relate them to your job situation, family, friends, cost of living, housing, and education. They are:

(1) things, people, or situations that in all probability will not have changed;
(2) things, people, or situations that in all probability will have changed; and
(3) things, people, or situations you wish would have changed during your absence.

In planning for possible problems, you are better prepared for handling the things that could go wrong. On the other hand, if there are no problems, or things have turned out better than expected, you have lost nothing in the process.

Ideally, the work of worrying should be carried out by the entire family. Quite often it is the wife who is responsible for keeping the family together during a move, and she must take it upon herself to go through the work of worrying alone. In some cases, a couple may go through a modified form of the work of worrying with each other but will fail to include the children. There is an unspoken belief that children should either not be exposed to unnecessary problems or be forced to face things when they come up. The assumption is that responses can be made at a later, more appropriate time.

Leave-taking, however, is a period marked by change, separation, and loss, and none feel it more than children. If children who are excluded from the work of worrying have problems in readjusting to school back home, they may feel they have failed or believe they are weak or unlike other children. If proper preparation is made, the entire family will be much less self-blaming and will realize that each child's response may be quite appropriate to the difficult situation.

Prior to departure, children between the ages of four and twelve may begin to act out by displaying aggressive or passive behavior, receiving poor grades, or reverting to bed-wetting, or they may experience nightmares. Adolescents may begin to feel anxious; feelings of fear, dread, or anger are particularly common during their last two semesters of school. In the adolescents' anticipation of the return home, schoolwork, extracurricular activities, time spent with friends, and their health may undergo profound changes.

Parents must be tolerant, sensitive, and nurturing during the time of moving and changing schools. Unfortunately, this is also the time when parents are equally stressed and preoccupied with their own set of problems. Regressive behaviors are a sign that the child needs a strong sense of reassurance. This is a time when the child should not be asked to meet the parents' needs by behaving like "big boys and girls" and staying out of the way of busy parents. Children need to be prepared and know what to expect. They should be allowed and even encouraged to express their feelings of helplessness, rage, and loneliness. It is also useful for parents to encourage children to talk about their fears and fantasies instead of letting them build up inside. Children's books on moving and separating from friends are usually available at school libraries and can be good triggers for beginning such conversations. Books for adolescents are also available.

A "moving workshop" is offered at some international schools for children who will be leaving Japan at the end of a semester or school year. At the workshop, children are encouraged to discuss their feelings about the upcoming move. They are encouraged to do their work of worrying by drawing pictures of what they will miss about Japan, what they fear about the new or old place they will be moving or returning to, and what will be nice about the new or old place. When children voice concern about whether they will be able to make new friends, they are gently asked how long it took them to make friends when they moved to Japan. Most will realize that it didn't take them that long, so they will probably be able to make new friends again rather quickly. Children from the ages of six to twelve commonly express the following concerns: Will my friends in Japan remember me? Will anyone like me in my new school? Will the new school be too big for me? Adolescents worry about the drug scene, safety, and peer acceptance.

The number of individuals who seek out professional help rises considerably during the winter months (January to April). In general, this phenomenon is attributed to the fact that many people have feelings of "being in the dumps" during these months. For expatriates in Japan, it is also a time when many of them are making preparations for their return home. Unknowingly, those who enter counseling with the hopes of "sorting through" some problem areas prior to their departure have already taken the first step in beginning the work of worrying.

Leaving Japan
There are some issues related to departure that may require of the returnee a little more effort and a greater coping capacity. What follows is a discussion of the most common reasons for leaving Japan and the specific issues that each may engender.
Visits Home Home leaves, furloughs, vacations, or sabbaticals—the much-welcomed trips home provide the expatriate with a chance to touch base with the home culture, renew old friendships, take care of extended family, and stock up on unavailable goods. They also provide the opportunity to make plans for the future, that is, look for a new home, evaluate schools, or look into new job possibilities. Most expatriates find that these regular, predictable, brief interludes help revitalize their waning spirits, giving them a boost to reenter life in Japan with zest. Some find home leaves unsettling, reopening many unresolved issues from the past or arousing negative feelings about living in Japan.

This one-to-three-month visit home is in many ways an unreal experience, as it allows the expatriate to focus on the best parts of the home country while ignoring the worst parts. This narrow view can, if not balanced with a realistic assessment of the total home situation, add fuel to the already existing high expectations often associated with a permanent return home. Even if the expatriate has had to confront some of the more unpleasant aspects of being home, there is a certain sense of detachment in knowing that one soon can and will be out of the situation.

Those who may have had an extended home leave (six months to one year) or furlough for the purpose of medical treatment, continuing education, taking care of family matters, or other reasons should expect to experience the processes of reverse culture shock to some degree. They should also expect some symptoms of renewed culture shock upon their return to Japan.

Fulfillment of the Assignment There are many reasons for returning to the home country, but perhaps the most common is the successful completion of an assignment. The most pressing problems that may arise for those who depart Japan for this reason are conflicts within the marital relationship and, for some women, in the area of work.

As discussed earlier, living in a foreign culture can exacerbate an ailing marriage. If marital difficulties were not dealt with during the stay in Japan, then the prospect of returning home brings back memories of the state of the marriage in pre-sojourn days. Unresolved issues, which were put on the back burner prior to coming to Japan and kept there throughout the overseas stay, press for recognition again. Issues such as a lack of communication and physical intimacy, differences in child-raising practices, and the lack of professional or personal common interests creep in as unwanted visitors and add to the overall stress of preparing for departure. This time, however, there is a sense of urgency in wanting to do something about the problems and a desire to seek the resolution of marital tensions prior to the return home.

The effort to deal with unresolved issues that arise at this time is further complicated by the upcoming move. Going home to an all-too-familiar place and situation may raise expectations about the outcome of the marriage to levels that are either unrealistically high or too low. It is not uncommon for couples to feel that this move will either bring them closer together or lead to divorce. The fact is that both partners will have changed to some extent as a result of having lived overseas, thus changing the dynamics of the marital relationship for both better and worse. It is essential that the couple planning to return home realizes that they cannot take for granted that either their spouse, their relationship, or their personal problems are the same as they were prior to coming to Japan. Pre-departure time offers not only a chance to discard some of the outdated marital baggage but a chance to appraise the new. For many, this can be a much-welcomed second chance.

For some returnees, especially those with marital difficulties, leaving behind the expatriate lifestyle may become an additional source of stress. This is especially true for those who have been able to keep a troubled marriage together simply because of the distractions of settling into a new culture and enjoying its many benefits, e.g., high job satisfaction and salary, the novelty of a foreign culture, new friendships. There is no doubt that the expatriate package can temporarily perk up a wilting marriage. In some cases, the return to their previous reality can seem like a cruel joke, especially if the couple has come to believe that the Japan experience has had a favorable impact on their marriage.

Workwise, while it is usually the husband who may have satisfactorily completed his overseas assignment, it is the wife who may leave feeling unfulfilled and resentful of having to leave a job that she may not be able to see to its completion. This is especially true for those who have invested a considerable amount of time and energy in building up a successful business or have put together a financially rewarding career in the field of editing, consulting, translating, or media work. Not wishing to throw away the many work-related contacts they have made over the years, an increasing number of women have begun to use their pre-departure time to prepare themselves and their Japanese counterparts to be able to continue their work via phone, fax, e-mail, and periodic visits back to Japan. Once back in their home country, many women have taken advantage of the resources found in groups that are specifically aimed at meeting the needs of returnees. Such groups are invaluable in helping to ease the repatriation process. One person we know started a group for women who have lived overseas, which includes citizens of various countries. The group engages in activities such as book readings, volunteer service projects, and international events. It provides an important forum where members can share and validate their experiences, and it also provides an arena for one's expanded interest in international topics. The group, which has grown by word of mouth from five to more than one hundred members, continues to flourish; it now has a monthly newsletter and looks forward to further growth.

Returning Early For families who decide to return before fulfilling their overseas assignment, the decision to leave Japan comes about after much anguish. The decision is usually made sometime during the first six months, after realizing that staying would be too great a sacrifice to either career (the job turned out differently than expected) or the family (children and/or spouse are unhappy), or because a crisis back home requires attention (the illness or death of an immediate family member). In most cases, however, returning early to the home country comes about when the gap between expectation and reality was indeed too great. Many of these families did not have the opportunity to come on a "look-see" trip prior to making a final commitment.

For these families, the return is often filled with mixed feelings—relief coupled with guilt and a sense of failure. The desire to just run away and forget "it" ever happened is a tremendous temptation. For many, coming to terms with their decision and the accompanying feelings is a necessary part of preparing to go home. Saying good-bye to newly acquired friends as well as to the positive aspects of their Japan experience help make for a smoother transition back home.

Returnees who have yet to complete the culture-shock phase are of the mind-set that once home, all will be "back to normal." Because of the high stress levels and emotionality that accompany a premature departure, returnees are more likely to experience some form of reverse culture shock. This can be avoided, however, if they leave with a balanced picture of both the positive and negative aspects of Japan and of the country and situation to which they are returning.

Abrupt Departure Sometimes the expatriate family is faced with having to make a premature departure because the employer may, without too much warning, order the family to either come home or go to another country. In most cases, this happens after they have finished the first three-year term and are well into the second term. Though there is usually some warning as to the possibility of moving, and though the family may plan for the day, it never quite looks or feels the same as they had anticipated.

All of a sudden, leave-taking becomes not a process but the end result. There is little time for the emotions, let alone the mechanics of moving. A wife's ikebana (flower arranging) course may never be completed, while the husband may have to face the prospect that he will never get to level four of *Nihongo* (a level of Japanese language proficiency). Although parents are usually more prepared for the move, children are often "yanked" out of school in mid-semester, having to make a hasty good-bye to friends, teachers, domestic help, and a country they consider home. There may not even have been enough time for friends and colleagues (especially during summer and winter vacations) to be able to put together a proper sayonara party. To help deal with the very real situation of being and feeling out of control, one veteran expat chose to host her own series of sayonara parties in order to have a sense of closure to all her relationships. Such self-hosted good-bye parties are equally important for children, who are not only faced with leaving behind their peer group but must also finish their education in a new school without immediately being able to make new friends.

Since there has been little time to prepare psychologically for the move, the central issue for those who leave under these circumstances is the burden of having to deal with unfinished business. Although you can tie up loose ends in personal relationships with the knowledge that there will be some sense of continuity via letters, e-mail, and visits, leaving behind unfinished projects can be much more difficult. Feelings of disappointment, resentment, anger, or sadness may crop up later, especially if a substitute for what was left behind is not found.

For those of you with little time to attempt anything resembling the work of worrying, reentry may be a time to get caught up and catch your breath. Remain mindful that you are going through two different processes at the same time, and then back off from becoming impatient with yourself and other members of the family. This advice also applies to families who, instead of returning to their home country, are asked to go to a new culture. They must simultaneously go through the process of leaving Japan and take on the task of adjusting to another foreign country.

Separation/Divorce Those who decide to leave Japan because of the dissolution of a marriage may do so abruptly. Such abrupt departures are often the result of finding out about a spouse's affair, or they may be due to physical or mental abuse in which the injured party is without separate living quarters or emotional support. Although many of the issues are the same as others who abruptly depart, there is also the additional high level of stress related to the breakdown of a marriage (see the Social Readjustment Rating Scale, p. 16). Nevertheless, it is important, even under these circumstances, to allow children to say good-bye to their friends properly and to attend to their emotional needs, despite the tumultuous nature of the departure.

On the other hand, the decision to divorce a Japanese spouse is often made after much thought and planning, as it may involve the lives of children who must adjust to a new culture, while the parent must readjust to a culture that may be equally unfamiliar. The task of understanding the legal proceedings in addition to the divorce and child-custody laws of both cultures may be a frustrating and time-consuming endeavor.

For the non-Japanese spouse, fears about returning home usually revolve around what to expect in terms of work opportunities, life as a single parent, and questions about how well they will fit socially back into their own culture after a long absence. However, because many have been doing the work of worrying over an extended period of time, they are usually able to make a fairly smooth transition back into their culture—much to their own surprise.

Death of a Spouse Of all the circumstances that can force one to leave Japan, perhaps no reason is more traumatic than the death of a spouse. For those sent to Japan for a contracted period of time, the sponsor will often handle the funeral and repatriation arrangements. Many expatriates find comfort in returning to their home country, where they can be with family and loved ones. The same issues facing those who must leave abruptly also apply for those who are forced to leave Japan as a result of a spouse's death.

Similarly agonizing is when the surviving spouse must decide whether to continue to live in Japan or to go back to the home country. Expatriates who find themselves in this situation are primarily those who are married to a Japanese national, gainfully employed, or are long-term or permanent residents.

Regardless of one's situation, it is important to realize that the death of a spouse has a value of 100 on the Social Readjustment Rating Scale (p.16). This means that any changes made during the first year or so may result in compromising one's own and one's children's mental and physical health. Therefore, it is advisable not to make any major decisions or changes with regard to selling property, moving or returning to one's home country, finding a new job, or placing one's children in an unfamiliar culture or school system.

Instead, this is a time to take advantage of one's support system in Japan, whether it be colleagues and friends, ties with various groups and committees, a religious affiliation, or one's Japanese in-laws—especially for the sake of the children. This is in spite of the fact that one's instinct is to flee from the place that is filled with both good and bad memories and is the source of overwhelming feelings of sadness, guilt, anger, and fear. By waiting out the year in Japan, the surviving spouses will be in a better position to decide what is best for them and their family. And if they decide to return to their home country, they will do so with a lighter heart, not having denied or delayed the grieving process.

Retirement Those about to retire and return home are confronting issues related to a major life stage (see page 16) in addition to dealing with reverse culture shock. In this situation, it is necessary to carry out the work of worrying for both retirement and repatriation. Some individuals romanticize both events as the much-awaited period in which they can do all the things they never had time for but will be able to do in their home country—the land they had always dreamed of returning to. For people who have spent much of their lives moving around and never owning a permanent home, the thought of being in one place for the rest of their lives seems like the next best thing to heaven.

The gap between expectations and reality, however, may be much larger than they anticipated. In addition to the normal sense of loss felt at retirement, expatriates from Japan may also feel the loss of the special *gaijin* status, work seniority, or the general esteem Japanese society has for the elderly. Many people experience the loss of long-term professional and personal contacts and a chance to use their knowledge of the Japanese language and culture. The networks and status they carefully built while living in Japan are sorely missed.

To help ease the trauma of this double transition, some opt to return to Japan to work under a different sponsor. Others begin a lifestyle that includes living in both Japan and their home country on a turnabout basis. Still others, though few in number, retire in Japan.

Being Home

Despite the many challenges posed by the repatriation process, a simple truth still exists: Although you may have left Japan, the Japan experience will not leave you. In effect, your sojourn continues.

Your ties with Japan will not be severed. Keeping up with friendships through correspondence and periodic visits, and retaining an interest and concern for what is happening in Japan via the media, bring home your continuing emotional investment in Japan. Events, both tragic and triumphant, will touch you in ways that would not have been possible before. Your school-age children may return to Japan on their own during the holidays to spend time with Japanese friends and their families.

Keeping up with your newly acquired interests will continue to expand your horizons. Your Japanese language ability, skills like ikebana and brush painting, or even the photographs you took can all be shared with others through classes, lectures, special-interest groups, and the written word. Your professional skills and experience can motivate you to maintain or further your study or training. After returning to your home country, you may find yourself launching a career as a cross-cultural trainer and consultant.

The sojourn continues because you have broadened your identity. Although a part of you may be content to pick up where you left off, another part will seek out ways to continue your participation in the international community. You could meet periodically with other returnees for a Japan Night, or join or start a group for other returnees. You might host a Japanese student, become involved in a local group for third-culture kids, or conduct orientation programs for local citizens who are moving to Japan or for Japanese who have come to your country to live and work as expatriates.

As Paul Tournier, a well-known Swiss psychiatrist, has so eloquently put it:

> All our experiences, emotions, and feelings are indissolubly linked in our memories with places. Man is not a pure spirit, and he has part in the places in which he has lived and experienced joy or sadness. He is bound up with matter, with things, with the ground he lives on. Our place is our link with the world.[6]

And, ultimately, being home is about feeling at home with our many selves. Welcome home, wherever you may be.

Afterword

Over ten years ago this book first appeared, in slightly different format, under the title *The Japan Experience: Coping and Beyond*. Since then, Japan has undergone significant changes, both economically and socially. While it was not long ago that Japan was considered to be an "economic miracle," today, in addition to dealing with the effects of the bursting of the bubble economy, the Japanese are having to adjust to numerous social changes, particularly in the areas of family, education, and work.

During this same time period, the expatriate community has also seen changes. For instance, before the late eighties, the American expat business sector consisted primarily of middle-aged family men with school-age children who were sent to Japan to fill upper-level management positions. Today, one is just as likely to see expats who are in their twenties and thirties, holding middle- or upper-level management positions, both men and women, single, and, if married, with either very young children or none at all. However, perhaps the greatest shift that has occurred during the past decade involves the location of the expatriate community. There has been an increase in the number of expats who are living or working outside of major cities and who involved with the Japanese community to a far greater extent than ever before. Furthermore, many more expats now possess Japanese language ability, both spoken and written. To some extent, many of these changes are not only a response to Japan's expectations and needs but a reflection of the economic and social situation back in their home countries as well.

Updating and revising this edition has meant taking into account many of the changes that have occurred over the years in both the Japanese and expatriate communities. It is interesting to note, though perhaps not all that surprising, that the kinds of problems encountered by expats living in Japan as delineated in our first book have, for the most part, remained unchanged.

The principal reason for this, as mentioned in the introduction, is that many of the problems faced by expats in Japan (and elsewhere) are related to an individual's or family's developmental-maturational stage. Although the stresses brought about by living in a foreign environment may trigger or exacerbate known (or unknown) preexisting personal, marital, or family difficulties, the human developmental experience in general seems to remain unaltered, regardless of physical location.

This explanation reinforces the often observed fact that while living in a foreign country may have its difficulties, it is usually not the culture per se that will be the main cause of an expat's problems. What may become problematic, however, is one's personal and culturally based reaction to and manner of dealing with those culture-specific differences. In fact, from all indications, any "other" culture seems to be fairly innocuous, especially since expats are usually not expected or required to become a part of it, at least to the extent that a native must. Rather, as discussed at length in this book, far more consistently predictable and often troublesome aspects of living in a foreign culture will more likely be those that are shared by expat communities worldwide, for example, experiencing culture shock and reverse culture shock.

For these reasons, this book will be useful to expats who are currently residing in Japan and who may also be anticipating another overseas assignment. Having an understanding of the expatriate experience in general, and more specifically of Japan, has helped departing expats to minimize (though not entirely alleviate) the uncertainty and apprehension of moving to a second or third culture, as well as helping reduce reverse culture shock problems.

AFTERWORD

To help further one's interest and knowledge about living in Japan or overseas in general, an Additional Readings list has been provided. While it is obviously not a complete list, it will give the reader an idea of the kind of books available and expose expats to some of the studies conducted with regard to living abroad.

Additional Readings

Albright, Sandra, et al. *Moving and Living Abroad: A Complete Handbook for Families.* Hippocrene Books, 1993.

Alston, Jon. *The Intelligent Businessman's Guide to Japan.* Charles E. Tuttle Co., 1990.

American Chamber of Commerce in Japan. *Living in Japan.* American Chamber of Commerce in Japan. Published annually.

American Citizens Abroad. *Handbook for Citizens Living Abroad.* Doubleday, 1990.

British Chamber of Commerce in Japan. *Japan Posting: Preparing to Live in Japan.* British Chamber of Commerce in Japan, 1990.

Community House and Information Centre. *Living in Kobe.* Community House and Information Centre, 1999.

Conquest Corporation. *Teen Talk: Straight Talk about Moving, One Teen to Another.* Conquest Corporation, 1993.

Eakin, Kay Branaman. *The Foreign Service Teenager: At Home in the U.S.: A Few Thoughts for Parents Returning with Teenagers.* Overseas Briefing Center, Foreign Service Institute, Department of State, 1988.

Ferguson, Paul, and Tom Boatman. *Networking in Tokyo: A Guide to English-Speaking Clubs and Societies.* Charles E. Tuttle Co., 1995.

Gerner, Michael, et al. "Characteristics of Internationally Mobile Adolescents." *Journal of School Psychology,* vol. 30 (1992).

Giardini, Alyson. "The Formation of National Identity Among U.S. Citizens Growing Up Overseas." Master's thesis, Stanford University, 1993.

Global Nomads: Cultural Bridges for the Future. Produced by Alice Wu, Lewis Clark, Marianne Bojer, and Illan Barzilay. Cornell University, 1994. Videocassette.

Hachey, Jean-Marc. *The Canadian Guide to Working and Living Overseas.* Intercultural Systems, 1998.

Hall, Edward, and Mildred Reed Hall. *Hidden Differences: Doing Business with the Japanese.* Anchor Press, 1990.

Intercultural Press. *Between Cultures: Developing Self-Identity in a World of Diversity.* Intercultural Press, 1996.

Janssen, Gretchen. *Women on the Move: A Christian Perspective on Cross-Cultural Adaptation.* Intercultural Press, 1992.

The Japan Legal Aid Association. *Living with the Japanese Law: A Guide to Foreigners in Japan.* The Japan Legal Aid Association, 1991.

Kalb, Rosalind, and Penelope Welch. *Moving Your Family Overseas.* Intercultural Press, 1992.

Kataoka, Kiroko. *Japanese Cultural Encounters and How to Handle Them.* Passport Books, 1993.

Kohls, Robert. *Survival Kit for Overseas Living: For Americans Planning to Live and Work Abroad.* Intercultural Press, 1996.

McCluskey, Karen. *Notes from a Traveling Childhood.* Foreign Service Youth Foundation, 1994.

Meltzer, Gail, and Elaine Grandjean. *The Moving Experience: Practical Guide to Psychological Survival.* Multilingual Matters Ltd., 1989.

Additional Readings

Oak Associates. *Japan Unveiled: Getting Acquainted.* Yohan Books, 1995.

Pascoe, Robin. *Culture Shock! Successful Living Abroad: A Parent's Guide.* Time Books International, 1992.

———. *The Wife's Guide to Successful Living Abroad.* Time Books International, 1992.

Piet-Pelon, Nancy, and Barbara Homby. *Women's Guide to Overseas Living.* Intercultural Press, 1992.

Romano, Dugan. *Intercultural Marriage: Promises and Pitfalls.* Intercultural Press, 1988.

Shepard, Steven. *Managing Cross-Cultural Transition: A Handbook for Corporations, Employees, and Their Families.* Aletheia Publications, 1997.

Smith, Carolyn D. *The Absentee American: Repatriates' Perspective on America.* Aletheia Publications, 1994.

———, ed. *Strangers at Home: Essays on the Effects of Living Overseas and Coming "Home" to a Strange Land.* Aletheia Publications, 1996.

Steinglass, Peter, and Martha Edwards. *Family Relocation Study: Final Report.* Ackerman Institute for Family Therapy for the U.S. Department of State, 1993.

Storti, Craig. *The Art of Crossing Cultures.* Intercultural Press, 1990.

———. *The Art of Coming Home.* Intercultural Press, 1997.

Taber, Sandra Mansfield. *Of Many Lands.* Foreign Service Youth Foundation, 1997.

Tokyo Union Church Women's Society. *Tokyo Tips.* Tokyo Union Church, 1996.

Wertsch, Mary Edwards. *Military Brats: Legacies of Childhood Inside the Fortress.* Harmony Books, 1991.

White, Merry, et al., eds. *Comparing Cultures: Readings on Contemporary Japan for American Writers.* St. Martin's Press, 1995.

Wood, David, et al. "Impact of Family Relocation on Children's Growth, Development, School Function, and Behavior." *Journal of the American Medical Association,* vol. 270, no. 11 (September 15, 1993).

Notes

Chapter 1
1. K. Oberg, "Cultural Shock: Adjustment to New Cultural Environments," *Practical Anthropology* 7 (1960), 177–82.
2. A. Furnham and S. Bochner, *Cultural Shock: Psychological Reactions of Unfamiliar Environments* (New York: Methuen & Co. Ltd., 1986), 47–50.
3. H. Higginbotham and J. Tanaka-Matsumi, "Behavioral Approaches to Counseling Across Cultures" in P. Pedersen, J. Draguns, W. Lonner, and J. Trimble, eds., *Counseling Across Cultures* (Honolulu: University Press of Hawaii, 1976), 263–65.
4. T. Takahashi, "Bunkakatto to Yamai" [Cultural Conflict and Mental Illness] in M. Iida et al. (eds.), *Seishin no Kagaku* 8 [Science of the Mind] (Tokyo: Iwanami Shoten, 1983), 209–96.
5. S. Aktar, "A Third Individuation: Immigration, Identity, and the Psychoanalytic Process," *Journal of the American Psychoanalytic Association* 43, no. 4 (1995), 1051–84.
6. Furnham and Bochner, 49–50.
7. Oberg, 177–82.
8. Express, semi-express, commuter express, and rapid express trains.
9. T. H. Holmes and R. H. Rahe, "The Social Readjustment Scale," *Journal of Psychosomatic Research* 2 (1967), 216. Used with permission of Pergamon Press.

Chapter 2
1. R. Conway, *The Psychological Effects of Cross-Cultural Experience* (Belgium: Université Catholique de Louvain, 1969).
2. C. Sluzki, "Migration and Family Conflict," *Family Process* 18, no. 4 (1979), 382.
3. Ibid., 385.
4. Maxine Gaylord, "Relocation and the Corporate Family," *Social Work* 24, no. 3 (1979), 186–91; quoted in Barbara Gewirtz, "Living Abroad: A Family Systems Perspective, Japan: Factors Which Affect Cultural Adjustment." Unpublished manuscript, 1981.
5. T. Fogarty, "The Distancer and the Pursuer," in E. Pendagast, ed., *The Family: Compendium II 1978–1983* (New York: Center for Family Learning,

1984), 45–50; and P. Guerin, "The Stages of Marital Conflict," in E. Pendagast, ed., *The Family: Compendium II 1978–1983* (New York: Center for Family Learning, 1984), 167–71. Information was taken from Guerin's article, which expands on Fogarty's concepts.

6. Fogarty, 169.

7. K. McCoy, *Coping with Teenage Depression: A Parent's Guide* (New York: New American Library, 1983).

Chapter 3
Diane Fassel, *Working Ourselves to Death* (New York: HarperCollins Publishers, 1990), 26–46.

Chapter 4
1. Ruth Hill Useem and Richard D. Downie, "Third Culture Kids," *Today's Education* (September–October, 1976), 103–05; Ruth Hill Useem, ed., *The Third Culture Children: An Annotated Bibliography* (East Lansing: Michigan State University, Institute for International Studies in Education, 1975); Ray F. Downs, "A Look at the Third Culture Child," *The Japan Christian Quarterly* (Spring 1976), 66–71.

Chapter 5
1. L. Pearlin and C. Schooler, "The Structure of Coping," *Journal of Health and Social Behavior* 19 (1978), 5.

2. Ibid., 10.

3. J. Pennebaker, J. Kiecolt-Glaser, and R. Glaser, "Disclosure of Traumas and Immune Function: Health Implications for Psychotherapy," *Journal of Consulting and Clinical Psychology* 56 (1988), 243–45.

4. J. Powell, *The Secret of Staying in Love* (Texas: Argus Communications, 1974; Valencia, Calif.: Tabor Publishing, 1974). Used with permission.

5. The Inventory of Personal Values was adapted from a cultural values worksheet that appears in David S. Hoopes, ed., *Readings in Intercultural Communication*, vol. 5 (Pittsburgh: University of Pittsburgh, 1976), 92.

Chapter 6
1. Based on a lecture given by Dr. John Kildahl in Tokyo (September 1980).

2. I. Skuja and J. Norton, "Counseling English-Speaking Expatriates in

Tokyo," *International Social Work* 25, no. 3 (1982), 30–42.

Chapter 7

1. R. Brislin and H. Van Buren, "Can They Go Home Again?" *International Educational and Cultural Exchange* 9, no. 4 (1974), 19–24.
2. C. Austin, ed., *Cross-Cultural Re-entry: An Annotated Bibliography* (Abilene: ACU Press, 1983).
3. N. Sussman, "Re-entry Research and Training: Methods and Implications," *International Journal of Intercultural Relations* 10 (1986), 235–54.
4. R. Brislin and P. Pedersen, *Cross-Cultural Orientation Programs* (New York: Gardner Press, 1976), 19–21.
5. Brislin and Van Buren, 21.
6. P. Tournier, *A Place for You* (New York: Harper and Row Publishers, 1968), 14.

Author Profiles

Joy Norton, an American, was born in Shanghai, China, and raised in Japan and the United States. She earned master's degrees in Asian studies and psychiatric social work from the University of Hawaii while at the East-West Center in Honolulu. She has authored several books on haiku and formerly served as a columnist for *The Japan Times*. A co-founder of Counseling International, she specializes in individual and marital therapy, in addition to career, cross-cultural, and telephone counseling.

Tazuko Shibusawa, co-founder of Counseling International, was born in Tokyo and raised in Japan and the United States. She received her master's and doctoral degrees in social work from the University of California, Los Angeles, and specializes in individual, couples, and family therapy. She is currently on the faculty at the Columbia University School of Social Work in New York, where she teaches clinical practice and conducts cross-cultural research among older adults and their families